ENDOR

"We've been friends with Brad and on the journey together pursuing a spiritual life with Jesus and one another for almost forty years. It's been an amazing trip! The thoughts and ideas in this book are ones we endorse for a young man's growth, really for any man's growth."

Dave, Tim, and Marty

"'Substantive,' Brad's book is that.

"I've known Brad since his sophomore year at Nebraska and watched his progress from a freshman in the basics of discipleship to a model disciple-maker of Jesus.

"Brad deals with the major matters of life in a fast, page-turning style. It's practical for any serious student of Scripture, whether he be on campus or in Congress. Study this book. Let its words transform you. Who knows what God might do through you."

Jim Hiskey, former PGA golfer, cofounder of the C. S. Lewis Institute, and author of *Winning Is a Choice*

"The thoughts and stories in *What I Wish I Knew in My 20s* reverberate with insights on faith, growth, and friendship. These messages of faith, love, and courage spur reengagement with the world around us and shed light on topics I wish I'd known more about in my twenties."

Steve Largent, NFL Hall of Famer and four-term US Congressman

"Brad and I have been friends for better than twenty-five years. We have shared a kindred spirit for working with men young and old to think about leadership and the thoughts of Jesus.

"Whether from our homeland in the Midwest or from the nation's capital, we have together witnessed lives changed for the better. I am strongly invested in the principles on which Brad expounds."

Clyde Lear, founder, Learfield Communications

"Over the past decade I've watched Brad Olsen disciple young men in the person of Jesus, guiding them through the various areas of life, which are both talked about regularly and, especially, those areas that are not.

"Now Olsen, who is an award-winning editor and former journalist, puts his hard-earned lessons on life and leadership on paper for all to read and examine.

"Let Olsen's *What I Wish I Knew in My 20s* serve as the foundation for future generations of young men searching how to grow into the leader and man that Jesus intended."

Andrew Marin, PhD, award-winning author of *Love Is an Orientation, Our Last Option,* and *Us versus Us*

"Brad's concern for the youth goes beyond the borders of North America to all the continents including Africa where he has inspired many people, including me.

"He has helped me found a college prep high school in Malawi to prepare students to be leaders not just of tomorrow but of today. I have learned, and continue to learn, a great deal from his leadership based on Jesus of Nazareth."

Joe Mtika, PhD, president and CEO, Norfolk Schools in Malawi Inc.

"In the whirling gyre of social debate about the need for a transformed male identity is a breath of fresh air in this age of gender revolutions from an author who has been in the trenches for four decades, this little book offers some much needed wisdom.

"His winsome tales of young men discovering their 'authentic self' beyond the politics and sociological currents of our age are refreshing.

"Olsen's wisdom-packed little book is a practical handbook for raising up the kind of 'adventurous' young men our chaotic world needs to inspire a new century with a grounded hope. It's a gem."

**Dr. William G. Nottage-Tacey, pastor emeritus,
First Presbyterian Church, Hastings, Nebraska**

"This long-overdue resource book is a gold-mine of practical, immediately applicable wisdom that will help the reader better understand himself, his life, his relationships, and his God. Brad speaks to the heart of the key questions young men are asking and what they need to know to become 'more than conquerors.'

"Based on my more than forty years as a theologian, seminary professor, clinical psychologist, including ten years of speaking for Promise Keepers to over a million men in stadiums across the country, it's obvious that Brad is addressing some significant core issues and concerns that every young man (and older man) faces. This is an invaluable resource that you will read more than once and recommend to your friends."

**Gary J. Oliver, ThM, PhD, clinical psychologist, executive
director for the Center for Healthy Relationships, professor of
psychology and practical theology at John Brown University**

"My son's book is accessible and exciting. It is a resource for both the young and old—including those of us who have accumulated wisdom over the years and want to place it in the hands and minds of the next generation! Is there a better gift? I can't think of any!"

Dr. Chuck Olsen, pastor and author of books on spiritual leadership

"Brad Olsen has spent most of his life working with Christian ministry on Capitol Hill. His experiences working with interns and members of Congress tell a very different story about life in our nation's Capitol than what most people hear and read. Brad is very well versed in Scripture and does a wonderful job of relating how Scripture impacts the lives of those with whom he comes in contact. I recommend his book without reservation. It will be enlightening and inspirational to the reader."

Dr. Tom Osborne, Nebraska football coach, College Football Hall of Fame, three-term US Congressman, cofounder of Teammates with wife Nancy

"Brad Olsen's *What I Wish I Knew in My 20s* is a treasure trove of wisdom from a seasoned servant of Christ. He provides insightful guidance to young men (and old ones like me) for traveling the path of sanctification and spiritual maturity. Indeed blessed is the man who walks in the counsel of this book!"

The Rev. Dr. David J. Peter, professor of practical theology, dean of faculty, Concordia Seminary

"I have utilized these teachings of Brad Olsen and his friends in building all my business interests. Brad has been a mentor, friend, and sojourner on many of my own adventures. I have always appreciated his thoughts and wisdom, especially how they have helped shape my leadership approach for my teams."

Toby Rush, general partner and managing director,
GroundTruth Studio

"Brad Olsen has inspired young leaders for decades with his passionate commitment to sharing and living the principles taught by Jesus of Nazareth. We believe this book will encourage and educate young people for years to come!

Jim and Linda Slattery
Jim: former six-term US Congressman, businessman, lawyer;
Linda: longtime mentor to college women with
National Student Leadership

WHAT I WISH
I KNEW
IN MY
20s

WHAT I WISH
I KNEW
IN MY
20s

A Life Manual for Men

BRAD OLSEN

ILLUMIFY MEDIA GLOBAL
Littleton, Colorado

REVOLWORKS PUBLISHING
Annapolis, Maryland

WHAT I WISH
I KNEW
IN MY
20s

Copyright © 2019 by Brad Olsen

Published by
Illumify Media Global and Revolworks Publishing
www.IllumifyMedia.com
"Write. Publish. Market. SELL!"

Library of Congress Control Number:

Paperback ISBN: 978-1-949021-80-6
eBook ISBN: 978-1-949021-81-3

Typeset by Art Innovations (http://artinnovations.in/)
Cover design by Debbie Lewis

Printed in the United States of America

To my wife, Beth, for her love, faithfulness, and patience

"A leader is best when people barely know he exists,
When the work is done, his aim fulfilled,
They will say, 'We did it ourselves.' "
— Lao Tzu, 565 BC

CONTENTS

FOREWORD

"Friendship is the greatest of worldly goods. Certainly to me it is the chief happiness of life. If I had to give a piece of advice to a young man about a place to live, I think I should say, 'Sacrifice almost everything to live where you can be near your friends.' I know I am very fortunate in that respect."

— *C. S. Lewis*

Friendship changes lives. More directly, friendship changed my life. I married my friend from high school, Terri, and we built our lives together. My teammate Jim Zorn and I became best friends during our years with the Seattle Seahawks, and our on-field chemistry culminated in more than a few league yardage records.

Without the friendships I was blessed with early on, and cultivated as I grew, I would not have much worth noting today: my marriage to Terri, our four wonderful children, their spouses and children, a spot in the NFL Hall of Fame, or my (four) terms in the U.S. Congress.

These achievements are the fruit of making friendships a focus in my life. While the career stats, or the polls, might be what history records as valuable, what the scoreboard or search engine doesn't show are the teammates and relationships that made any move—in family, football, or politics—possible.

My relationships have at times proved painful. When I was six years old, my father left my mother and her three sons. Recovery from that traumatic experience challenged me and advanced my desire for loving and faithful relationships.

In my work with young people over the years, I've witnessed several societal evolutions. Friendship as we know it is changing. Technology and entertainment are altering the ways we seek, and sometimes find, connection. Numerous studies show correlations between social media use and its effects on mental health. This data, though ironic, is not new. More recently, however, research has established a stronger link between social networking and social anxiety.

A recent University of Pennsylvania study, published in the *Journal of Social and Clinical Psychology,* shows that limiting social media use to thirty minutes a day helped people feel "significantly better." The bottom line, according to the author of the study, is "using less social media than you normally would leads to significant decreases in both depression and loneliness."[1] The human connection we seek, once thought to be facilitated by technology, actually becomes hindered by it.

Yet supportive relationships are more important than ever, as young adults (eighteen- to twenty-five-year olds) in particular are faced with making decisions that lay the foundation for the rest of their lives. The pressure these massive decisions exert, when faced alone, can lead to the anxiety and depression plaguing young people today.

Relationships were an integral part of the life of Jesus. He lived on the road with a team of His own: twelve guys with their own flaws, doubts, and failures. Yet just being around Him, serving Him, was somehow powerful enough to make them put aside their differences (as best they could) while He built His network of friends and followers on earth. Now we are called to do the same.

The thoughts and stories in these pages reverberate with insights on faith, growth, and friendship. They encourage us to consider our relationship with God, our relationship with others, and our relationship with ourselves. These messages of faith, love, and courage spur reengagement with the world around us, shedding light on topics I wish I'd known more about in my twenties.

— *Steve Largent*

Inductee, NFL Hall of Fame

Four-term U.S. Congressman

ACKNOWLEDGMENTS

First and foremost, I'm forever grateful to Jesus, for His love, faithfulness, and patience. I'd also like to thank my beloved wife, Beth, for her love, faithfulness, and patience. And I'm grateful to Chuck and Joyce Olsen, my parents, who turned my life into a schoolroom for growth, and my children and their spouses, for their support. Much gratitude to Jeremy, Macarena, Ben, Libbie, Holly, Matt, Dawson and Meila (and granddaughters Sloan and Ana); my assistant, Hollis Barth Brandon, for the contribution made with her immense talent; my tsunami of friends, especially those who specifically encouraged me to write: George, Marty, David, Tim, Gerard, Bob, Mike, Ed, and Clarke. And I thank any persons willing to pick up this book and expose themselves to its inherent risk. You are the true heroes.

PROLOGUE

Marvin Martin knew about life. He spent most of it as a labor lawyer in Wichita, Kansas. During his tenure, he had a front-row seat to human nature in all of its best and worst portrayals. Later in his life, his children and grandchildren begged him to write a book, filled with the wisdom that he had shared with them through the years.

He wrote the book called *Four Generations: A Journey Through Life*. I had the great fortune of reading it and asking him questions. There was one thing Marvin mentioned that I'll never forget: Every young man needs a great adventure between the ages of eighteen and twenty-five. The boldness of men's lives will be determined by the boldness of their adventures.

He went on to talk about the "greatest generation." This generation of young Americans lined up to enlist to fight on one of the two fronts to bring down fascist dictators.

We all know the history. The Western Allies won the war, both in Europe and in the Far East. What we have been too quick to forget is the amazing contributions that this generation made after the war.

They were the fathers of the baby boom. They moved America to the forefront in business and industry. They took it upon themselves to rebuild their enemies, Japan and Germany, an effort unparalleled in history.

And they built. They built bigger homes, factories, cities, and the like. They invented at a frenetic pace, constantly raising the standard of living.

Whenever I think about Marvin, it leads me to think about Teddy. Born to a wealthy and influential family, he grew up in New York City in the late 1800s.

Not only did his father lead the company and create a future for the city, he was also an every-Sunday Sunday school teacher. From him, Teddy learned about business, history, society and what it meant to be a man of faith.

Teddy's family bought several houses that they set up as lodging for newsboys. These young men and boys, mainly orphans, made their scant living hawking newspapers on the streets of New York City.

These houses were the first stop on the family's Saturday routine. In the morning, Teddy and his family would tromp over to one of the homes and spend a couple of hours eating breakfast and playing with the boys.

Later in the morning, they would visit the Metropolitan Museum, which their family had helped found. Then they went over to Central Park, where they enjoyed their picnic lunch. The rest of the day was free, aside from a few chores that needed to be done, so that they could set apart Sunday for their rest.

When Teddy was a young man, he was somewhat sickly. His father suggested an unusual prescription for Teddy's severe asthma. He had Teddy exercise and do everything he could to make himself physically fit. Oddly enough, it worked. Teddy overcame his frailty, and even spent two years in the Badlands of South Dakota (known as "the Dakota Territory" at that time), working as a wrangler on a ranch.

During Teddy's school years, his father took the family out of school and spent two years touring Europe, Northern Africa, and the Middle East. Tutors traveled along to help the children with their studies.

Yes, Teddy's was a life of privilege. That's not the point. He lived a life full of adventure like few people I know.

During his life, he led the "Rough Riders" on their travails in Cuba during the Spanish-American War of 1898.

He loved the Navy and supported it. Teddy's voice was boisterous. He lived a big life for all to see. Indeed, he was bigger than life. His fans loved him, and his detractors hated him for the influence he wielded.

You probably know the rest of the story. Teddy became President Theodore Roosevelt, the twenty-sixth president of the United States. As president, he continued his adventurous life with great effect.

He spoke eloquently and often about life. Here's a sample from a presidential campaign address in 1898:

> A soft, easy life is not worth living, if it impairs the fibre of brain and heart and muscle. We must dare to be great; and we must realize that greatness is the fruit of toil and sacrifice and high courage. . . . For us is the life of action, of strenuous performance of duty; let us live in the harness, striving mightily; let us rather run the risk of wearing out than rusting out.

In today's age of absent or divorced parents, addictive video games, and cell phones that turn us into zombies, we need more Teddys.

xxvi   WHAT I WISH I KNEW IN MY 20S

This book is about becoming a Teddy. Wouldn't it be great if there was a renaissance, where young men became reattached to society in a way that would turn it upside down?

Such is the vision of Jesus. His teachings stretch us all to great lengths, but at the same time, cause us to grow through the challenge, pain, and suffering.

This is a book that I hope will catapult young people into a search for adventure, and ultimately, a life lived with significance.

I hope you enjoy reading these thoughts. My closest friends and I have been teaching them for more than forty years. Yet the wisdom is much older than that, and we are grateful that it has been passed along so faithfully through the generations.

We have used many instruments as we work with young men and young women. The latest are an international prayer convention and various student gatherings on the topics of faith and values.

So read these points, ponder them, discuss them with your friends, and if you find that they have merit, work them into your life. A word of warning: some of these matters are deep ones. I suggest reading only one or two segments a day, or better, read them with someone else.

1

LOVE

Love: The greatest happiness of life is the conviction that we are loved, loved for ourselves, rather loved in spite of ourselves.

—**Victor Hugo**

B efore we build anything, we must discuss the world's most necessary ingredient. The apostle Paul sets the standard for any good work. He touts the currency we call love. Without love sprinkled throughout our actions, we are nothing, he wrote in his first letter to the Corinthians.

Let's stop for a second and digest this.

Nothing at all that is any good can be done without love. Really?

We do all kinds of things that seem good, progressive, and important. But we often do them out of fear, judgment, jealousy, malice, or insecurity. At the end of any day, when we check our conscience, how much were we motivated by love? It's a good question. If we can get over the fact that we have heard so much about love, we realize the incredibly powerful nature of the message. The only real currency that bears good fruit in life is love.

Nothing at all that is any good can be done without love.

Love has powers of its own. It has density. Perfect love can overcome fear. In our scariest moment, the thought of love can bring us peace. Can you imagine that? So when we feel fear, it should be an invitation to recall and remember how much love the Father God has for us. So then, the one who fears does not really understand love. We can only truly love when we first understand that we are loved.

Embracing the Love of God

Receiving the love of God proves tricky. We think we understand God's love for us and that we truly believe it. Yet in a moment of insecurity, we revert to fear and disbelief. Try an experiment. Ask people on a scale of 1 to 10 (with ten being very good) how good they are at believing God loves them.

Over the past few years I asked people this question, and all but three gave me answers five or below. One said seven, and two said ten. The two who said ten claimed they simply chose to believe, just like a child believes, that he or she is loved. This proves reminiscent of Jesus' observation that the wise miss things, while children can simply embrace them.

It's too bad there aren't more techniques for childlike faith, but it seems that God impresses people personally and uniquely of His love for them. He reveals it over and over, then asks us to simply believe.

Imagine a football game. Each play starts with one simple maneuver: the center must give the ball to the quarterback. If the center does not perform this all-important function, the play is destined for failure. The quarterback must first receive the ball before he can do anything. He can't run it, he can't throw it, he can't pitch it—nothing.

Likewise, we can do nothing unless we first receive the love of God.

Jesus said that we should care for our neighbor. An obvious problem surfaces: How can we possibly love another person unless we ourselves have received the self-sacrificing love of God?

Paul writes, "that you, being rooted and grounded in love, may have strength to comprehend with all the saints what is the breadth and length and height and depth, and to know the love of Christ that surpasses knowledge" (Eph. 3:17-18). This becomes a starting point for life.

How do we embrace the boundless capacity of God's love for us? If we can receive it, much like the quarterback receives the football, everything else happens automatically.

One friend loves to say, "We need to stop thinking we can do something for God to love us more." This sounds good but proves difficult in practice. We think that if we perform a certain way those around us will be impressed and like us more. Such an equation does not work with God. He already loves us more than we can ever imagine. This should provide security and a strong foundation on which we can stand.

Onlookers should look at us and notice that we care for each other. According to Dutch Catholic priest and theologian Henri Nouwen, this should be our "distinguishing trait."

One way to understand love is to study its opposite. Most people think the opposite of love is hate. But with hate, we require energy to use against a foe. No, the opposite of love is indifference, in which we couldn't give a flip about what happens to another human being.

What, then, does it mean to love? Love requires that we place the needs of others before our own. When we do so, our motives should be pure. In other words, we should expect no repayment, no reward, no accolades.

We tend to think, "Well I did such and such for so-and-so. Why won't he or she give back to me?" Once again, selfishness rises to the fore. We need to stop thinking about what we can get back and contemplate what we can give, if we are to follow Jesus' example.

One question cuts to the quick, "Am I a net giver or a net taker?"

When we walk into a room, are we looking for opportunities to give or opportunities to take? In any given relationship, are we net givers, or net takers?

Identifying great givers proves challenging, as truly great givers give without drawing attention to themselves. They seamlessly assess needs and find ways to quietly meet them. More on giving later.

Here's another thought from Henri Nouwen: "May all your expectations be frustrated. May all your plans be thwarted. May all your desires be withered into nothingness, that you may experience the powerlessness and poverty of a child and sing and dance in the love of God the Father, the Son, and the Spirit."

Self-Giving Love

The English language has no counterpart to *agape*, the Greek word for self-emptying love. This is the love that puts the needs of others before our own. Matthew wrote that we should gather this sort of love for God first, then for others, even as we learn to love ourselves.

When John writes that God is love, we realize that love is a person.

So how does a person love God? Well, it starts with a quick study of what He says He wants from us. We love God first by receiving the fact that He loves us. This is a concept that we cannot grasp until we feel as a parent does toward his or her children.

My friend David has a question he asks kids of just about any age. "Why did your parents have you?"

The responses are widespread:

-- "Because they wanted my help."
-- "Because they were lonely."
-- "Because that's what married people do."
-- "Because my older sister wanted a sister."
-- "Or simply, and most often, "I don't know."

Few get the right answer: Most parents simply want to love someone made in their likeness. It is natural. God Himself made man in His image, and man became the recipient of God's great love. Ever since, there is something about loving another human, especially one made in our likeness, that connects us to God Himself.

Once I was playing golf with a recent high school graduate. I asked him, "What is the purpose of life?" He shanked the next three shots. He came from a Catholic family. I knew his parents. But he had no answer for my question. When he asked for the answer, I told him, "You need to do the homework on this one. Go back and ask your parents. Then ask your teachers and your priests." I never heard back from the young man, yet I remain curious about how his conversations went.

Someone asked Jesus once what the greatest commandment was:

> And he said to him, "You shall love the Lord your God with all your heart and with all your soul and with all your mind. This is the great and first commandment. And a second is like it: You shall love your neighbor as yourself. On these two commandments depend all the Law and the Prophets." (Matthew 22:37-40)

Think how easy it would be if we only had to remember two things to fulfill our purpose in life. Jesus requires that we think like children, so He made his teachings plain and simple. Yes, plain and simple, yet virtually impossible. So He gives us a lifetime in this earthly classroom so we can learn how to receive God's love, to return it to God, and then to allow it to spill over onto those around us.

Recipients of Agape

When my children were young, I used to love to take the older ones to play golf. One day, I was playing with Jeremy, ten, and Ben, eight. I was a bit distracted because I was trying to think of the best way to tell Jeremy that I wanted to take him to his first Nebraska Cornhusker football game the following Saturday.

I have heard it is a bit difficult for others to understand this crazy religion that we call Nebraska football. Young Nebraskans dream of the day that they will be taken to Memorial Stadium, a.k.a., the Temple, where strong young men have played the game for well over a century.

Jeremy was old enough to take his first trip to Lincoln for a big game.

On the first hole of our golf game, Jeremy had a nice shot into the green that stopped twelve inches from the hole. Excited for him, I blurted out, "Whoever makes the next putt gets to go to the Nebraska football game with me next Saturday!"

In hindsight, it was stupid and insensitive. I hadn't really noticed, but Ben's errant chip shot had sped past the hole and had come to rest about twenty-five feet behind it. Given my earlier announcement, of course, Ben fell to the ground weeping, knowing that he faced an impossible putt, while Jeremy's was a tap-in.

Ben gave it his best try, spending at least five minutes lining up his twenty-five-foot, double-breaking putt. Finally, he addressed the ball, lined up his putt, and struck it. It rolled down the left side of the green, crossed to the right side, then back toward the left. Coming out of its break, the ball straightened out directly toward the hole with the perfect speed. It rimmed into the hole and back out, resting one inch away.

Ben again crumbled to the ground, sobbing. Meanwhile Jeremy, distracted by the drama, nearly missed his one-foot putt.

Words cannot describe how it feels as a father to injure your own child. I had hurt Ben deeply while trying to bless Jeremy.

We played a couple more holes, but the shadow of Ben's disappointment hung upon us all. Finally, we opted to call it a day and drove a golf cart back to the parking lot. The three of us drove in silence for the five-minute ride back to our house. When we arrived home, I went upstairs to dress for dinner. As I wondered how I could redeem the awkward event, a knock came at the door. It was Jeremy.

"Dad, I think Ben wants to go to the game more than I do. I think he should have my ticket."

I started to argue with him, when the realization struck me that Jeremy was extending to his brother the kind of love that trumped everything.

"So do you want to tell him, or would you like me to?" I asked.

"I'll tell him," he said.

Jeremy left the room, and I could hear him going downstairs to the kitchen. I heard some murmur of conversation and then a scream. Ben came running up the stairs, jumped into my arms, and told me that he would be going to the game with me on Saturday.

God found a way to bless all three of us. We call that redemption: the Lord takes our garbage and turns it into gold.

Over the next few days I realized that this must be how God feels when His children care for one another. I am grateful that God redeemed the awkward situation, but I am more deeply touched that I was able to catch a glimpse into the way God feels about us.

When we care for those around us, we should feel God's pleasure. I was even able to take Jeremy to another game later in the season.

We also must realize that this self-giving love will cost us something. It will, and it should, hurt. We cannot care for others unless we are willing to let go of something or to expose ourselves to pain or loss.

This exposure can look as dramatic as dismantling roadside bombs, or as subtle as relinquishing the rights to a football game ticket. Self-sacrifice reverberates from the phrase "I volunteer as tribute," etched into our minds by the *Hunger Games* series. While the story offers many examples of selflessness, the starkest comes early on when the township selects its annual contender for the Games, a gladiator-type survival tournament. When Primrose Everdeen's name is drawn and blared over the loudspeakers, Katniss Everdeen runs forward and volunteers in her stead, taking her younger sister's place and thereby facing almost certain death.

This willingness to relinquish, or to suffer, is ultimately how we find fulfillment. We receive by giving. We are healed when we are hurt. We appreciate what is true when we understand how it feels to be told a lie.

This is how we grow.

Loving Your Rivals

God desires, no, requires, that His people love everyone. We try to sneak around this point, making excuses to exempt ourselves. "That guy did this and that, so I can write him off," we often say to ourselves. But then we realize that God says we need to love our neighbors.

"Well, I've lived my whole life with my brother, and I am tired of him." Jesus requires that we love our brothers.

"This person is a complete jerk and has gone out of his way to be my arch-enemy." Jesus also requires that we love our enemies.

Unfortunately, we can't find any way to wiggle off the hook.

I once saw this principle implemented to great effect. Each Sunday evening I met with a small group of men. We were

pressing one another to grow spiritually and to learn how to
love better. One Sunday, Mike, a golf pro, entered the room
with a noticeable spring in his step.

"What's up, Mike?" we asked.

"I finally got the votes on the board to throw Chuck out of
the club," he boasted.

Chuck was a member of the golf club at which Mike served
as head pro. Chuck had complained about Mike ever since
he came to the club. Whatever Mike tried to do, Chuck was
pulling the other way. And complaining. Mike was delighted
that, with the board of directors' backing, he was finally to be
rid of his nemesis.

A question came into my mind that I couldn't help but
release: "So if Jesus wants to teach us how to love our enemies,
what makes you think God won't put another jerk in your life
once Chuck is gone?"

Mike looked shocked. He'd never thought of it that way. As
we discussed the idea, we asked him, "If there was one thing you
could do to show Chuck love, what would that be?"

Mike immediately cradled his face in his hands and slowly
shook his head back and forth.

"I can't believe I'm going to do this," he wailed.

We all wondered what Mike could possibly be thinking.

In those days, every Monday the pros would take their
favorite members to a pro-am tournament somewhere in the
state. It always involved beautiful golf courses, competitive golf,
plenty to eat and drink. It was every member's dream to be
invited.

"I'm going to take Chuck to a pro-am next week," Mike
announced with a reluctant tone.

When Mike asked Chuck the next day to go to the pro-am, Chuck was floored. He could not possibly have seen the invitation coming, since he'd been Mike's antagonist since the two met. He quickly accepted.

The following Monday, my buddies and I were all wondering how Mike's day had gone. When we met at the club on Tuesday for our normal Stag Day event, Chuck happened to meet us at the door.

"How was the pro-am yesterday, Chuck?" we asked.

Chuck couldn't stop talking about his experience, his newfound friendship with Mike, and the great talks they had on the car ride to and from the event. As the weeks went by, we saw that somehow Chuck's outlook on Mike, on the club, and on life, seemed to have been lifted. All by a simple invitation to play golf.

Have we ever thought what it would be like to do the kindest thing we could imagine to the person who deserves it least? Such is the way Jesus lived and taught. And He asks it of us.

Think for a moment what the world would be like if everybody went around looking for ways to please their worst enemy. Of course, this scenario is wildly improbable, perhaps ridiculous. But wouldn't it be worth a try? Can it start with us?

Jesus had in mind that His followers would be marked, more than anything else, by love. Over and over, He reminded us how we should love God, love ourselves, love others, and yes, love our enemies.

BELIEVE

~

Things are not as they seem. We think that our five senses pick up everything. Not true.

According to the apostle Paul, invisible things last forever while visible things will come to an end. We tend to obsess over cars, clothes, professional titles, careers, checking account balances, and other things that make us feel secure.

But Paul stretches us. He contends that invisible things—prayer, connection with God, character, relationships, thoughts, motivations, love, mercy, redemption, salvation, heaven, God Himself, and the list goes on—prove to be more valuable. These are the things that make this world go around.

At one point the disciples asked Jesus, " 'What must we do to be doing the works of God?' Jesus answered them, 'This is the work of God, that you believe in him whom he has sent' " (John 6:28-29).

Jesus turns our idea of work upside down. It's not the heavy lifting achieved via our brains and brawn but our hidden life of faith that is important. One cannot read this dialogue between the disciples and Jesus without looking inward and wondering, "How much energy do I exert to believe in Jesus? Do I even know how?"

Thinking about this, I recently adopted a mantra. I was once challenged by my father (a lifelong pastor whom I respect) to develop a mantra for my breathing exercise that I could think alongside my breathing in and out. My mantra goes something like this: "Rest in the things of Jesus (exhale) and believe (inhale)."

When one thinks about the work of God, the last thing that comes to mind is rest. Our American culture catapults us into the world of heavy labor. We strive and exhaust our energy attempting to impress God (or people) with production or performance.

Yet God feels no different about our efforts than He did toward the people of Babel as they constructed a tower to reach upward. They believed that their works could build them the proverbial highway to heaven. God thwarted their efforts by confusing their languages to prevent another such prideful display. He witnessed and understood the power of mankind's unity—for good and evil.

This book seeks to squarely challenge young men to live abundant lives full of faith. Of course, all of us need to admit how badly we fail at this. We are constantly distracted by worries and wealth. When worries surround us and press in, we see less and less of Jesus.

Yet in the midst of chaos and distraction, Jesus calls us out. He tends to first turn our lives upside down and then challenges us to refocus on Him.

2

PRAYER AND GIVING

Be not forgetful of prayer. Every time you pray, if your prayer is sincere, there will be new feeling and new meaning in it, which will give you fresh courage, and you will understand that prayer is an education.

—Fyodor Dostoyevsky

I t is hard to imagine any relationship that is not founded on good communication.

So how good is God at communicating with us?

There is a plethora of tools God uses to communicate with His children. He speaks to us in the Scriptures. He speaks to us in His creation. He speaks to us through others. His very spirit lives in our hearts and carries on daily dialogue. He speaks to us through experiences. He speaks to us in great books. He speaks to us as we worship. He speaks to us in solitude, prayer, and meditation. Some have verbally heard His voice. He comes to us in our dreams. His spirit guides us at every turn. When it comes to communication, God is clear and all encompassing.

The real question becomes, "How well do I listen?"

The best illustration of this is the radio tower. Day and night, hour after hour, any given radio station pumps out its programming from high and powerful towers. The signals seldom waiver. When we tune in our radios, the programming pours through.

God is the radio tower. He communicates powerfully and personally to every individual whom He loves. Meanwhile we, His distracted followers, march through life entranced by the millions of interruptions that blast into our brain uninvited.

The very complexity of the society in which we live dictates that we must hear and process hundreds of messages every day. Somehow we need to find solitude. And when we do, we hear God's still small voice chiming in. It's as if we just tuned our radio. The static disappears. God's clarity has a chance to reach us.

One mentor of mine likened our brains to a computer. Any computer is only filled with what has been put in it. So when you extract information from the computer, you only get out what has been programmed inside. "Garbage in, garbage out," our computer science teachers always told us.

So we should be careful about the things we invite into our minds.

We should fill our minds with beautiful thoughts, both ours and others'. Collect quotes. Keep track of your favorite stories. Work up your own illustrations based on various truths. Think positively about those around you. Your mind will become the palette from which God will paint your life.

Constant Prayer Works

Jesus was surprisingly specific when He taught His disciples how to pray. According to Him, we should believe while praying; we should pray in agreement with others; we should pray constantly; we should ask boldly; we should ask persistently; we should pray as a child does; some prayers are only answered when accompanied by fasting; we should pray using His name; we should pray in secret; we should pray for laborers to build the Kingdom of God; He gives us a prayer to imitate; and we should pray for those in authority.

God is fully interested in our lives, and in the lives around us. He wants to be involved. He listens. His communications are mostly clear. And when they are not, we should wait for clarity.

Let's be clear on this: Our Maker wants to have an intimate relationship with every one of us.

> **Our Maker wants to have an intimate relationship with every one of us.**

Jesus said, "Abide in Me as I abide in you. Just as the branch cannot bear fruit by itself unless it abides in the vine, neither can you unless you abide in Me. I am the vine, you are the branches. Those who abide in Me and I in them bear much fruit, for apart for Me you can do nothing." (John 15:5)

Really? . . . "Nothing?"

"Nothing" here means nothing of eternal consequence in my best definition. An apple tree branch can only produce an apple if it draws nutrition from the ample resources of the tree's root system. So we, too, succeed only when we rely on the resources of the Almighty.

Here is what the apostle Paul told believers in Thessalonica: "Rejoice always, pray without ceasing, give thanks in all circumstances; for this is the will of God in Christ Jesus for you." (1 Thess. 5:16-18)

Have you ever wondered what God's will for your life is? You need look no farther than the preceding paragraph. To call this idea a challenge is to completely underestimate its difficulty. The exhortation is simple but most improbable.

Brother Lawrence took on this challenge literally as described in the book *Practicing His Presence* by Brother Lawrence and Frank Laubach. Here is what Brother Lawrence wrote about his experiment:

"We are to make a great difference between the acts of understanding and those of the will. Acts in response to our own mental understanding are of comparatively little value. Action we take in response to the deep impressions of our heart are all of value. Our only business is to love and delight ourselves in God." This requires constant spiritual concentration.

Let's stop here. Do we really think it suffices to simply "love and delight ourselves in God"? Can it really be enough?

Brother Lawrence found God in the dirty dishes. Can we?

When confronted by the Pharisees, Jesus spoke of the two great commandments and said, "By these two are all the laws and the commandments fulfilled."

If nothing else, the Jews were experts at making laws. In total, more than six hundred laws were imposed on the Jews by their religious leaders. Jesus sliced through all this clutter and got right to the heart issue. If humans could only learn to love—including God, our neighbor, and ourselves—everything else would become second nature. All the commandments, including the Ten Commandments, would be fulfilled. The Ten Commandments concern themselves with how we relate to God (firstly) and how we relate to one another (secondly). So even the tablets of Moses adopt these two ideas as primary.

It seems that Job One is to love. Anything without love is fruitless, just as anything without God is fruitless. In order to move on, we must never forget our highest priority: letting love live through us.

CHAMBERS ON PRAYER

Oswald Chambers has impacted my thinking on Jesus and prayer like no other person. In his now-famous devotional, "My Utmost For His Highest," Oswald Chambers outlines dozens of approaches to prayer. Here is a collection of them:

March 20: Think of the last thing you prayed about—were you devoted to your desire, or to God? Determined to get some gift of the Spirit, or to get at God? "Your heavenly Father knows what things you have need of before you ask him." The point of asking is that you may get to know God better. "Delight thyself in the Lord; and He will give thee the desires of thine heart." Keep praying in order to get a perfect understanding of God himself.

March 30: Are we worshiping? Or are we in dispute with God—"I don't see how you are going to do it." This is a sure sign that we are not worshiping. When we lose sight of God we become hard and dogmatic. We hurl our own petition at God's throne and dictate to him as to what we wish him to do. We do not worship God. Nor do we seek to form the mind of Christ.

May 26: We think rightly or wrongly about prayer according to the conception we have in our minds of prayer. If we think of prayer as the breath in our lungs, and the blood from our hearts, we think rightly. The blood flows ceaselessly, and breathing continues ceaselessly; we are not conscious of it, but it is always going on.

August 28: Prayer is the life of God nourished. Our ordinary views of prayer are not found in the New Testament. We look upon prayer as a means of getting things for ourselves; the Bible idea of prayer is that we may get to know God himself.

September 12: Stand off in faith believing that what Jesus said is true, though in the meantime, you do not understand what God is doing. He has bigger issues at stake than the particular things you asked.

September 16: Get an inner chamber in which you pray where no one knows you are praying, shut the door and talk to God in secret. Have no other motive than to know your Father in heaven. It is impossible to conduct your life as a disciple without definite times of secret prayer.

October 11: If God has given you a silence, praise Him, He is bringing you into the great run of His purposes... If Jesus Christ is bringing you into the understanding that prayer is for the glorifying of His Father, He will give you the first sign of His intimacy—silence.

October 17: Only a child gets prayer answered; a wise man does not... You labor at prayer, and results happen all the time from His standpoint. What an astonishment it will be to find, when the veil is lifted, the souls that have been reaped by you, simply because you have been in the habit of taking your orders from Jesus Christ.

December 13: As a worker, be careful to keep pace with the communications of reality from God or you will be crushed. If you know too much, more than God has engineered for you to know, you cannot pray, the condition of the people is so crushing that you cannot get through to reality.

Made in God's Image

"In the image of God he created him; male and female he created them" (Gen. 1:26). This verse has puzzled many. How can we understand what it means to be made in God's image when we can't even see Him? We are physical creatures, and physicality plays an enormous role in our grasp of reality. It is no wonder that Israel worshiped the golden cow, nor is it surprising that remote civilizations built idols to their gods.

Through the ages, man has worshiped just about everything: plants and planets, trees and animals, mythical figures, a mother goddess, and even the dirt. We were born to worship. Left to ourselves, we will find something to idolize. Even today, we worship money, the human body, celebrities, and politicians. We just can't help ourselves.

So isn't it interesting that the Scriptures tell us that man was made in the image of God? Jesus takes it one step further. He says, "as you did it to one of the least of these my brothers, you did it to me." (Matt. 25:40).

How practical is that? We can actually worship God and/or Jesus by the way we treat one another. You see, the way we treat our fellow earth-mates proves sacred when we realize that he or she is made in God's likeness. God takes this personally.

Pray for the Poor, the Hungry, and the Alien

Carlos led me on one of my greatest adventures. I met him while preparing for a student gathering for our state. A group of college students and I had been to a student meeting in Washington, DC, in the early 1990s. The seven of us were inspired by it and set out to pull off a similar experience in Lincoln, Nebraska.

The group met diligently to plan all the details: the dates, venues, the invitation list, the small-group facilitators, the speakers, and even fun time. We began our efforts in the fall for the weekend conference the following spring.

The committee worked diligently to hammer out the details of the event, including asking then Gov. Kay Orr to host the event, along with other political figures and state leaders.

We made hundreds of phone calls to recruit college leaders to come to Lincoln for the weekend. Everything seemed to be falling together.

As the list of attendees grew, we wondered about something. Sure, forty or fifty students had verbally committed that they would come. But no one had paid, and few had returned the RSVP included in the invitation.

We backtracked to make sure those who had committed were actually coming. To our chagrin, no more than twelve students were committed. We had already reserved rooms at the Cornhusker Hotel, which was then Lincoln's finest and most expensive hotel.

We had planned room assignments and meals for the larger number. The hotel stood firm that we were obligated for rooms and food for forty, so we met to decide what to do about our financial crisis.

A crazy idea came up. "Because we are already going to lose our shirts on the forum, why not fill the hotel and deal with the money later?" someone suggested. It was like Jesus' parable of the wedding banquet held by the king. In the parable, the invited guests all replied with excuses. One had farm work, another had business to attend to, and some even killed the king's servants (Matt. 22:1-10). So the king told his servants to go out and invite the people from the streets. The new guests were brought in, given wedding clothes, and the party ensued.

Our committee decided to do the same. Each of us did what we could to drag our friends and acquaintances to the event. We were marginally successful. The event, it seemed, was to be a wholesale bust.

Thursday came, the day everyone was to arrive at the hotel. I packed for the weekend and set off for the two-hour drive to Lincoln. I was haunted by the financial situation that would be hanging over our heads following the event. I was making a mental list of people who could help raise money to cover the shortfall.

"Why didn't you help us more, God?" I asked with equal parts anger, confusion, and fear. "Why have you left us dangling like this?"

Just then, I came over a rise in the road near Madison, Nebraska, home to a smelly hog processing plant. I noticed a young Hispanic man hitchhiking. He probably worked at the plant.

A car was stopping to pick him up when my instincts kicked in. I pulled in behind the other car and threw the door open to block the young man from getting into the other car. I'm sure Carlos was astounded that two cars were competing to give him a ride. It must've felt like a good day.

Carlos sat down in my passenger seat, and I pulled out onto the highway. I tried to explain the dilemma of my committee to him. We simply needed some people to come to our event. With his broken English, he tried to understand what I was saying. In the end, we agreed to the following (I think):

- I would drive him to his home in Columbus (a half hour away) to get his clothes. Since he needed a suit and tie but had none, I called my wife and asked her to bring my smallest suit, shoes, and a tie (and as many safety pins if she could find).
- He would come to the event and participate.
- His registration costs would be covered.
- I would find people who would translate for him.
- Afterward, I would give him a ride back to Columbus, and we would be friends.

So Carlos came to our event. An older and braver student, Damon, (was) volunteered to room with Carlos. The suit arrived via Beth, and we spent the better part of an hour pinning it up on a short young man who couldn't have been more than four feet ten inches. (I am five ten.) Ted and Josh, two students who grew up on the mission field in South America, volunteered to shadow Carlos, translating everything that happened for him.

The weekend started with a recreation night at the University of Nebraska football team's indoor practice facility. We set up our games in the cavernous hall. Most of us played soccer on a full-length field. Carlos, Ted, Josh, Damon, and a couple of athletic girls, Dawn and Jennie, led a spirited game.

Carlos seemed to be enjoying his new adventure. He was becoming the star of the weekend. Everything was going well— until Sunday morning.

The governor had addressed the participants on Saturday night. She enjoyed it so much that she made a surprise appearance at the Sunday morning brunch. As I entered the hall, I looked in horror across the room to see Governor Orr in the middle of what seemed to be an intense and confounding dialog with Carlos.

The next thing I knew the governor was making a beeline for me. I was sure she would demand to know why Carlos was there since clearly he was not a college student.

Sure enough, she asked me to explain. So I told her the whole story: the planning, the failed invitations, our plan B, picking up Carlos on the side of the road, and how it was going for him during the weekend conference. She hung on every word. When I was done explaining, I awaited her reply.

"So who is paying for him?" She asked pointedly.

"I don't know," was all I could say.

"Would you let me pay for him?" she asked with a smile.

She pulled out her purse, sat down, and wrote a check to cover Carlos' cost. I found out later that Carlos was not his real—or only—name. He was an illegal immigrant from Central America. Over the course of the next several years, he would show up at my office every month or two with details of where he was and what he was doing. He moved about the country finding work where he could. We always talked about the student weekend, and I couldn't help but smile at the irony that our governor unwittingly had helped finance him.

Our group was able to find some generous souls, who covered our losses that weekend. Our annual event lasted another ten years, with varying levels of participation. But when we talk about it, we always remember Carlos and his lasting impression on us.

I often wonder if he was an angel.

> **When we reach out to the disinherited in prayer and giving . . . we become the agent, the conduit of God's grace.**

The point of the story is this: When we reach out to the disinherited in prayer and giving, the Lord smiles on us. We become the agent, the conduit of God's grace.

"As you did it to one of the least of these my brothers, you did it to me," Jesus told His disciples (Matt. 25:40).

I was taught the importance of giving back by John Staggers, Tom Skinner, and the Rev. Sam Hines, three leaders who improved the District of Columbia bit by bit, one block at a time in the early 1980s. I was privileged to spend a summer on their staff, working alongside inner-city teens doing renovation work in beaten down housing in some of the worst parts of the city.

The people at One Ministries, as they called it, tried to pair urban churches with suburban ones in outlying Maryland and Virginia. The churches would build bridges with each other, which included regular workdays in the dangerous and scarred inner city.

We worked between Fourth Street, Third Street, M and N Streets in the Northwest part of the city. Fourth and M was a major drug trafficking corner. The Black Panthers hung out on nearby Ridge Street. It was a tough neighborhood.

Staggers, a former Marine and staff member for the mayor, could often be found on the block, chatting with neighbors or finding odd jobs for the community's many volunteers.

On Wednesdays, Rev. Hines, Staggers, or Skinner presided over the weekly prayer breakfast, which could just have easily been attended by a US senator as a homeless person. There was a powerful love on the Block, as we called it.

"Remember," John would remind us incessantly, "these people are Jesus to us. When we meet them, we meet Him. The way we treat them, we treat Him."

Seeing Jesus in Others

Jesus is available to us.

William Barclay, Scottish minister and theologian, says it best in his commentary on the Gospel of Matthew:

> There were two men who found this parable blessedly true. The one was Francis of Asissi; he was wealthy and high-born and high-spirited. But he was not happy. He felt that life was incomplete. Then one day he was out riding and met a leper, loathsome and repulsive in the ugliness of his disease. Something moved Francis to dismount and fling his arms around this wretched sufferer; and in his arms the face of the leper changed to the face of (Jesus).

> The other was Martin of Tours. He was a Roman soldier and a (believer). One cold winter day, as he was entering a city, a beggar stopped him and asked for alms. Martin had no money; but the beggar was blue and shivering with cold, and Martin gave what he had.

> He took off his soldier's coat, worn and frayed as it was; he cut it in two and gave half of it to the beggar man. That

night he had a dream. In it he saw the heavenly places and all the angels and Jesus in the midst of them; and Jesus was wearing half of a Roman soldier's cloak.

One of the angels said to him, "'Master, why are you wearing that battered old cloak? Who gave it to you?" And Jesus answered softly, "My servant Martin gave it to me." When we learn the generosity that without calculation helps men in the simplest things, we too will know the joy of helping Jesus Christ himself.[2]

The Art of Giving

Jesus wants us to give. There are few other issues into which He inserts Himself so personally. When we feed the hungry, when we give drink to the thirsty, when we invite the stranger in, when we clothe the naked, when we visit the sick, when we meet with prisoners, we feel His presence.

We need to understand four points about Jesus' view on giving and the poor:

1. He says we will always have the poor with us (John 12:8).

2. He alone is Jehovah Jireh, the Lord God Provider (Gen. 22:14).

3. He decides who gets what in this world, because it all belongs to Him (Ps. 50:10).

4. When we give to the needy, we meet Jesus face to face (Matt. 25:40).

It's hard to imagine that there's any way for Jesus to make it any clearer. An intern recently asked why God would allow some people to be poor and others to be wealthy. A good question. The answer is difficult to embrace: He does it because He wants to.

As hard as it is to imagine, the Lord puts poor people on Planet Earth so that we can have the opportunity and privilege of giving unto Jesus. He decides who gets which resources on Earth, and we decide who gets resources in heaven. What we do here determines our lives there (Matt. 6:19-21).

He also ordains some to have wealth, although nothing that they manage actually belongs to them. The Scriptures clearly teach that all the world belongs to Him. He created it, and He assigns stewards over it.

Admittedly, most of our giving is reactionary. Someone asks for something, and we decide, usually in the blink of an eye, whether or not to respond. Wouldn't it be more appropriate if our giving was proactive? What if we actively sought out those in need and creatively, along with the Holy Spirit, fashioned a suitable response?

Then we should ask ourselves:

"Am I giving from my excess or from my poverty?"

"Does it hurt when I give?"

"If it doesn't cost me anything, is it really giving?"

No one would criticize a person for giving out of his or her excess, and great things have been accomplished from wealthy people who never felt what it means to give until it hurts.

Wouldn't it be better, though, if we actually felt a shortage of something when we give? Jesus Himself chose a poor station when He was on Earth. Few of us think about the fact that Jesus never revealed what He would eat the next day. He didn't seem to know where He would sleep or if He would have shelter. And day to day, He relied solely on His Father to provide for Him and His disciples.

Jesus sets up instructions for us when we think about giving. First, when it is possible, it should be anonymous. Second, He teaches that we should use wealth to make friends. Third, He gave graciously of His time in order to grow people around Him.

And in our giving, we need to consider how the recipient might feel. It is entirely possible to demean someone in our giving. We should not give to make others feel dependent or to destroy their initiative.

While visiting Malawi in 2006, we were able to witness a feeding operation by an international relief organization. Because the country was enduring a terrible draught, people were streaming into the relief camp, leaving their homes behind.

It was explained to us that many who came to the camp would not be able to return to their homes. They were actually giving up their livelihood to get food for a few days. We had few better ideas, but we could see that the feeding camp was no long-term solution.

Alternately, we visited a few villages that had received a water well and pump. The well allowed villagers to grow a few crops and enjoy good drinking water. Perhaps this was a better long-term solution.

As we left one of the villages, we noticed that one pump's handle was lying on the ground because a small cotter pin had broken. The use of the expensive well had been shut down by a broken fifty-cent cotter pin. The well seemed a better solution, but not a perfect one.

Some people get confused about how much they should be giving. Jesus told a story about a rich young ruler. The man came to Jesus and asked what he should do to inherit eternal life. Jesus told him, Do not murder, Do not commit adultery, "Do not steal, Do not bear false witness, Do not defraud, Honor your father and mother" (Matt. 10:19). The man quickly responded, "All these things I kept from my youth."

The man claimed he met every benchmark necessary. One gets the feeling that Jesus was taken aback by his response. So Jesus, as He did from time to time, went for the proverbial jugular: "You lack one thing: go, sell all that you have and give to the poor, and you will have treasure in heaven; and come, follow me."

Just by reading the passage, one can feel the man's ego deflate. He walked away sorrowful.

We have all heard preachers talk about this so-called standard set up by Jesus. A few are quick to say that we should sell everything we have and give it to the poor. Yet Jesus only told this to one person. And it was in response to the man's asking to be made perfect.

It is clear from other references that Jesus never intended for every one of His followers to sell everything they owned. Yet he did insist on wholehearted commitment. This is what the rich young ruler lacked, and Jesus exposed him.

We find another troubling story of Jesus when we read about Lazarus. A certain wealthy man walked past the wretched beggar Lazarus every day without ever paying him mind. Yet Jesus says that in all eternity, Lazarus would be the one to sit at Abraham's side, and the rich man would be destined for the abyss.

Why does Jesus use such harsh scenarios? The truth is He cared enough about people to tell them the truth, then He died to remediate any deficiency in their existence.

The reason giving is important for us is that it was important to Jesus. He cared much less about what the recipient did with the gift than He did about the condition of the giver's heart.

Once again, Jesus wants us to care about the things that He cares about. He wants to take care of His people and meet their needs, and He wants us to care for people and meet their needs. It is one more factor that helps us to relate to Him in kind.

On Outgiving God

Giving requires artistry and is repaid lavishly by God.

When I was five, my allowance was ten cents a week. My mother gave me a nickel and five pennies each Saturday. The first penny was put in a jar to go in the offering basket in church the next day. So from a young age, I learned that the whole ten cents belonged to God, and I was the steward of the remaining nine cents.

Later in life, my wife Beth and I decided that the 10 percent tithe was not really giving, but rather returning a portion to the owner. We decided to challenge ourselves to give more, and to give in a way that we could actually feel the pinch. Some years we gave up to 50 or 60 percent. But there was a problem with this: God always gave us much more back than we gave.

If you want to try a fun experiment, try to outgive God. Beth and I tried, but we failed. Every time we gave what we thought was a ridiculously large amount, somehow God returned much more, and in shockingly creative ways. He has sent us cash windfalls, unsolicited donations, unexpected stock dividends, unthinkable stock appreciation, loans paid back that we had given up on, and the list goes on.

This little competition goes on, but let's just say that God has a lengthy lead.

Since the Lord deals with every man uniquely, I would add one caveat: God may or may not repay everyone the same way, but He guarantees that He will provide for His children all that they need.

3

REDEMPTION

Redemption: If the Father deigns to touch with divine power the cold and pulseless heart of the buried acorn and to make it burst forth from its prison walls, will He leave neglected in the earth the soul of man made in the image of his Creator?

—*William Jennings Bryan*

Everybody probably has heard of Humpty Dumpty, the egg who fell off the wall, broke open and couldn't be repaired. Who of us can't relate to the idea of feeling broken—so broken that nobody can put us together again? When a person is broken, he or she feels empty, lost, directionless.

We have all been broken. It is in the depths of this despair that God does His best work. When God sees something broken, He can't help but put it back together. And somehow when He puts it back together, it's better than before.

Perhaps the best metaphor for this idea comes from a Japanese form of pottery called Kintsugi, which means "golden joinery."

Legend has it that a fifteenth-century Japanese Shogun sent a cracked pot to China to have it repaired. When it was returned, the Shogun was disappointed to find that the mending consisted of unsightly metal staples.

This inspired the Shogun's craftsman to mend the broken bowl with fine gold. The craftsmen figured out a way to turn a broken pot into a breathtaking piece of art. The former defects, while still visible, were completely transformed. Gold shone forth from every crack.

God does this with us when we are broken. As we watch God do this in lives, one after another, we realize that somehow the broken people are better than before when they're put back together by Him.

Don't ask me how to explain this great dichotomy. Yet when we meet a new person, if we speak of our brokenness, our failures, our shortcomings, our mistakes, it draws the other person closer. If we brag about ourselves, talk about our trophies, our successes, our wealth, our physical fitness, somehow it alienates the other person, pushing them away. They want to do nothing but escape the conversation. It turns them off.

When I think about redemption, I think about Gus. I met him at a student gathering, and he and I landed in the same small group. To begin the weekend, we told our stories. Gus told a story I'll never forget.

His father and mother met at a bar one night, resulting in her pregnancy. She chose to carry her baby for nine months and give birth. After a year, she realized that the responsibility was too much for her. So she found the birth father and turned Gus over to him.

Gus's father was no saint, but he raised Gus as best he could. Gus made it through high school and was working his way through college when I met him. As our group met we challenged him to find his mother and thank her for giving him a life.

About a week later each one in the group received a text message from Gus. At the top of the message was a picture of him hugging his mother. She smiled broadly and proudly. It was a beautiful image.

For me this defines redemption. Despite our fumbles, bumbles and shames, somehow God turns them into something wonderful. I can't wait to hear what will happen in the years ahead with Gus and his mom. Their reunion was a gift from God.

The Gift of Vulnerability

Brené Brown, professor at the University of Houston, has made a name for herself writing and speaking about vulnerability. She makes the case that when two people meet at their least common denominator, a spark can start a friendship growing like a fire.

> **Our willingness to be vulnerable attracts others.**

Our willingness to be vulnerable attracts others. It draws people in. They can relate to us . . . finally. So what if we went about putting our humble foot forward rather than the prideful one?

What if we, as Jesus said, humbled ourselves that we might be exalted, rather than exalting ourselves that we might be humbled? What if we actually did sit at the end of the table in the seat of least honor, rather than jockeying for the seat of highest honor. How would it feel to be moved up to the seat of honor?

Or from another angle, how would it feel to be removed from the seat of honor and sent to the low end of the table to make room for a more deserving person?

Think if you will, with all your imagination, what amazing form Jesus could have taken had He wanted to. Why did the Father not insert Him into twenty-first-century America, where He could drive a Maserati and give rock concerts with amazing speeches to millions of followers? Why did God choose a meaningless town in a meaningless era in a meaningless outpost of the Roman Empire?

Perhaps it was because He wanted us to have the same attitude that was in Jesus, who, taking the form of a man,

> did not count equality with God a thing to be grasped, but emptied himself, by taking the form of a servant, being born in the likeness of men. And being found in human form, he humbled Himself by becoming obedient to the point of death, even death on a cross. Therefore God has highly exalted him and bestowed on him the name that is above every name, so that at the name of Jesus every knee should bow, in heaven and on earth and under the earth, and every tongue confess that Jesus Christ is Lord, to the glory of God the Father. (Philippians 2:5-11)

So, according to Paul, it was actually the fact that Jesus was willing to be humbled that He was given the name that is above every name. So it was because Jesus took the lowest station that He was given the highest one.

Perhaps Brené Brown got it right.

So what does this look like in real life? When we're in a conversation, do we make it always about us? Are we able to get over the "me" and onto the "you" and take a sincere interest in another person's life?

Can we actually put our pride in our pocket and wholly give our attention to someone else? Perhaps we could take an entire evening and do a crash course to learn more about our new neighbor. Or perhaps, are we willing to cancel our own plans to help a friend prepare for a job interview? We will get little to no attention for our deed, except in the sight of the Almighty.

The entire miraculous process of redemption begins at the breaking point: the day or hour when we discover, in no uncertain terms, that we are broken—undeniably. We are fallen beings never able to reach perfection on this side of heaven.

As the sober reality of our actual fallen state sinks in, God does something amazing. He reaches down, touches us, and makes us into something special: something we never could have imagined without Him. His will merges with ours, and the impossible comes into our sights. We can actually walk, step by step, in the sacredness of knowing our own weaknesses and at the same time understanding the rapture of exaltation.

Seeking the Divine Reset

Like an old computer that needs a reset to return it to the factory settings, a divine reset is when we return to our "factory" standards. Sometimes we have to hit rock bottom before we can be reset. Yet we seldom see the gift that lies there. As we walk through life, we routinely stumble, with our failures ranging from subtle to spectacular. Usually, we can recover. Yet there are times when we hit a low point. We look around, and there is no way out. That is rock bottom. Many members of Alcoholics Anonymous can speak on the value of hitting rock bottom.

At a men's meeting once, the leader asked everyone to share the most gracious gift that God ever gave them. Of the nine people in the room, four were alcoholics. Every one of the four knew exactly what their greatest gift was: hitting rock bottom.

There at the bottom is when the prophets of old would cry out to God to be rescued, or better, to be redeemed.

Dozens upon dozens of references throughout the Scriptures talk specifically about when a character reaches the bottom and cries out. For example:

> "The people of Israel groaned because of their slavery and cried out for help. Their cry for rescue from slavery came up to God. And God heard their groaning, and God remembered his covenant with Abraham, with Isaac, and with Jacob. (Ex. 2:23-24)

> "Then we cried out to the LORD, the God of our fathers, and the LORD heard our voice and saw our affliction, our toil, and our oppression." (Deut. 26:7)

> "Then they cried out to the LORD in their trouble, and he delivered them from their distress." (Ps. 107:6)

Most often, the Lord responds quickly to the cries of His children. In some cases, however, He requires them to wait.

We see this most poignantly in the story of Job. When Job reached the end of his rope, he cried out, but God did not provide instant relief. Instead, the Lord took His time responding to Job's cry. "I cry to you for help and you do not answer me; I stand, and you only look at me" (Job 30:20).

We should humble ourselves from time to time and admit that we have found a dead end and can see no way out. When we cry out, our voices go directly to the throne of God, whose deepest desire is to save us. Sometimes we have to wait, as Job did. Sometimes our help comes immediately.

When Jesus told the story of the prodigal son, we can visualize the loving and faithful father, who, seeing his wayward son in the distance, runs with all his might to go out and hug his returned child.

When Jesus told the story of the shepherd and the lost sheep, one can feel the tension of a shepherd who leaves the entire flock to save one missing sheep.

God grants us parenthood, so we can experience the urgency of our child who cries out for help, even as Peter cried out, after attempting to walk on water and sinking into the sea.

Racing to Rescue the One

One summer our large family was making its way through Disney World on our way to one of the theaters. On our way into the show I counted the group and came up one short. I realized I had left my eight-year-old daughter, Holly, behind.

We had both used the restrooms, and I had told her specifically that when she came out, she should wait at a certain spot and not move until I returned. I had been distracted by my task of herding the group to the theater and somehow assumed she was with us. Some fifteen minutes after my agreement with Holly, I was running with all my might from the show to return to the meeting point. I prayed with all my heart that she would be safe, that she would not get lost in the multitude of people who were milling about throughout the park. As I came around a corner, sweating and sprinting and out of breath, I looked ahead and there she was, my faithful daughter, doing exactly what I had told her.

It's hard to imagine feeling any greater urgency than when rushing to find your lost child.

I believe God gives us experiences like these so we can understand how He feels. I imagine Him sitting on His throne and feeling a rush of urgency when He hears the cries of His children.

It's critical that we understand this part of God. He loves us. He cries out to us in return. He drops everything to rush to our rescue.

> God loves us. . . . He drops everything to rush to our rescue.

Andrew, John, and Linda

We always wondered how my nephew Andrew had so much love for anything with wheels: tractors, trailers, cars, trucks, motorcycles—you name it, Andrew loves it. A few years ago, he began trading his vehicles online. He traded a scooter for a motorbike for a car for a better car for a truck and then for a front-end loader. Then he would start again: a motorcycle for a car for another truck, and so on. Now, at the age of twenty-five, he owns a nice fleet of vehicles.

God seems to always have a purpose. In the spring of 2019 our hometown, Norfolk, Nebraska, was threatened by a hundred-year flood. The levee held in Norfolk, but substantial flooding swamped the entire northeast region of the state. I tried to think of a way to help out.

A couple days later, I happened to see on Facebook that my twenty-five-year-old nephew, Andrew, had taken time away from his mowing and snow removal business (which happened to be sort of slow in March) to take vehicles filled with supplies to the victims of the devastating flooding near Verdigre, Nebraska.

Soon after, I saw a picture of Andrew with a small trailer loaded up to go. After hearing news of his efforts, people were sending thousands of dollars to him. He was converting the money into supplies and driving them to Verdigre. He even teamed up with a tractor supply company that gave him access to more trailers. Thousands of dollars continued rolling in.

Andrew had built relationships with a number of farmers in the Verdigre area, who directed him to the people in the most need. A week later, he was still going back and forth between Norfolk and Verdigre, trucking supplies to people (and cattle) in need.

I know Andrew well enough to know that if I asked him how he was inspired to help these people, he, in his ordinary Midwest way, would simply say, "It just seemed like the right thing to do."

How available are we for such inspirations?

In the late 1990s some former student friends of mine were married in Virginia but decided to drive the country for their two-week honeymoon. When they heard that there was flooding on the Missouri River in Omaha, they called us, asking if they could stay at our house and help with the flood damage.

So John and Linda stayed with us in our Omaha home, found a farmer who needed sandbagging, and worked for several days to help him hold off the floodwaters.

Who does this? Well, in this case, it was a man and his bride who care deeply about others. In the last year, John was chosen to be the US Ambassador on Trafficking in Persons. He has aggressively pursued and prosecuted human traffickers around the world. He's been a volunteer, a lawyer, a consultant, a prosecutor, and now an international leader on perhaps the greatest issue of our day.

What made him and Linda become interested in helping others? I'm not sure he can explain it, nor can I. Maybe "It just seemed like the right thing to do." Thank God that John and Linda are listening.

Stories like this abound. I loved, when working as editor of the *Bellevue*, Nebraska, *Leader*, when one of these stories walked in the door. We did all we could to get it on the front page, so people could see the "real news."

Andrew, and John and Linda are just examples of the kinds of inspiration that God gives us when He redeems our lives. Indeed, God takes our biggest pains, our biggest failures, and uses them for His own good.

We should remain open for the inspiration to help others, as He has helped us.

4

MYSTERY

It is impossible to account for the creation of the universe, without the agency of a Supreme Being.

—George Washington

Did God really create everything in six days?

Could a couple eating a piece of fruit mean the total and complete fall of man?

Did Joshua really defeat the Canaanites by circling the city, yelling, and blaring trumpets?

Was Jesus really born of a virgin?

How big is the universe? How can it still be expanding?

How do God's providence and man's free will converge?

These topics confound my mind. I simply can't get my brain around them.

When we consider the Scriptures, do we see them as purely concrete truth or as heavenly mystery? Perhaps the answer is Yes.

So we see that Scripture is filled with truths, and we attempt to stuff every one of them into our puny human brains. Often we miss the truths of Scripture because we argue vehemently about whether or not the narrative is true. The main points are lost in the squabbling over minutia. Wisdom is sacrificed for facts. The meat is discarded for the bones.

God is undaunted. He assures us, "My ways are higher than your ways, my thoughts above your thoughts" (Is. 55:9, NLT).

When we claim that we understand God and all His creation, it is as if an ant were bragging about his understanding of the planet. As focused as we may be, we are still small parts in the large puzzle. Small but loved. God is not operating on our scale. Just look through a telescope. We need to keep our knowledge in perspective—we are small parts of a gigantic creation. But we have hope that when the New Jerusalem comes, we will be given new bodies to scale new heights, eyes to see in the presence of brilliant light, ears that will hear the thundering beauty of God's voice, and yes, brains, to comprehend all that is true and important.

As Paul wrote, "Now [we] know in part; then [we] shall know fully, even as [we] have been fully known" (1 Cor. 13:12).

Believing in God

Ever since Adam and Eve sinned, work has become a curse to us. Indeed, it defines us. So through the ages, we have set our hearts on achieving our value through work.

If we fast-forward to the time of Jesus, His disciples, too, were enamored with the idea of achieving meaning through work. They came to Jesus asking how to do the works of God. Their focus was on the word *do*, as in what actions they needed to perform.

Jesus' answer is telling. He told them to believe!

This response puzzles us. Isn't sweat required to have true work? Don't we need a task list to complete? Don't we have to labor physically? At the end of the day, shouldn't what we possess have been gained through our work?

True work requires working alongside Jesus.

With Jesus, we can do "all things" (Phil. 4:13), and without Him we can do nothing (John 15:5).

Believing in Others

In what's known as the love chapter, Paul writes to his friends in Corinth that love "believes all things" (1 Cor. 13:7). Does that mean we need to believe in other people? Even though we know that they will lie and disappoint us just the way the disciples disappointed Jesus?

Russian novelist Fyodor Dostoevsky famously said, "To love someone means to see him as God intended him."

> **"To love someone means to see him as God intended him."**
>
> — **Fyodor Dostoevsky**

To put this into an equation, the authentic self, for any person, equals what people see themselves to be plus what others see them to be. So the difference between what another person is and what that person can be is sometimes the faith that we have in him or her.

When my kids were in grade school, I decided to believe them as much as possible, even when I guessed they might be lying. I gave them the benefit of the doubt. In some cases it meant I had to believe potential lies over a period of time. I wanted to convince my children that I believed them, and that I believed *in* them.

This obviously created pain for me and their mother—and for them. I continued to believe them during their years at home. I think the exercise was worthy. I believe my children grew to believe in themselves, and they believe that we believe in them.

As we work to convince others that we believe in them, hopefully they also come to believe that God believes in them. This is the ultimate work: to believe that our Maker Himself loves us and believes in us. So the question really becomes, are we willing to believe in other people the way that God believes in them?

Despite their infidelity, their falsehoods, their rejection, and their disappointment, can we still believe in them?

God tells us that He will take care of the rest.

Sports are chock-full of underdog stories. Surprisingly, the common denominator in the teams that overcome the odds is not height, nor speed, nor size. Rather, it's someone—be it a parent, a coach, or a player—who believes in the improbable in a way that changes the team, and therefore, the game.

Michael Oher was born one of twelve children to a father who was in and out of jail and a mother who was ravaged by addiction. Michael's childhood was fragmented. He was shuffled between foster homes and was sometimes homeless. He attended eleven schools in his first nine years as a student.

Needless to say, his performance at school suffered. He grew quiet and despondent. When Michael was sixteen, his estranged father was murdered. Michael was homeless at the time, though still attending high school. By many standards, his life was hopeless. That is until he was taken in by Sean and Leigh Anne Tuohy who saw him walking on the side of the road one night.

When the Tuohy's took Michael in his GPA was 0.06. Despite the intimidating incline of this uphill battle, they insisted on getting him a tutor to help with his grades.

With love, tutoring, and a warm place to sleep, Michael's performance improved to the point where he became eligible to compete in athletics. With the encouragement of Leigh Anne, he tried out for the school's football team.

Big for his age, Michael had been scouted by the gangs of North Memphis when he lived on the streets. His size made him ideal for a guard. Football became an outlet for him. At first, the coach struggled to find a position that maximized his speed and size.

Again, Michael grew despondent and discouraged, though Leigh Anne knew playing on the team would make a real difference in his life. After watching a few dismal practices, as the movie portrayed it, she observed that Michael might be better suited as left tackle, the one who protects the quarterback's blind side.

She crafted her pitch based on her knowledge of Michael's fiercely loyal temperament when she said:

> Now, y'all would guess that more often than not, the highest paid player on an NFL team is the quarterback. And you'd be right. But what you probably don't know is that more often than not, the second highest paid player is, thanks to Lawrence Taylor, a left tackle.
>
> Because, as every housewife knows, the first check you write is for the mortgage, but the second is for the insurance. The left tackle's job is to protect the quarterback from what he can't see coming. To protect his blind side.[3]

Something clicked. When the coach finally tried Leigh Anne's suggestion, they were shocked at the results. Michael made play after play, relentlessly defending his teammate.

In a memorable exchange between mother and coach, an incredulous Coach Cotton asks, "What did you say to him?" Leigh Anne responds, "You should really get to know your players. Michael scored in the ninety-eighth percentile in protective instincts."

His 0.06 GPA jumped to 2.5. A downtrodden homeless teen became a beloved member of a caring family. A struggling JV player became an all-American left tackle, who later became a starter for the Baltimore Ravens, winning the Super Bowl in 2013.

The difference between the former and the latter? The power of believing in the undiscovered value of someone else. Belief reveals hidden potential. Belief catalyzes transformation. We are all on the verge of our next level. Whom will we choose to elevate?

Calling Mother Teresa

Consider a story about a friend, Bart, from Santa Barbara, California. He and his small committee of Presbyterians were thinking about the 1988 General Assembly of the United Presbyterian Church-USA, which would be held in St. Louis.

One of the daunting issues of the General Assembly was to discuss the church's official view on abortion. Clearly, they thought, this could be a divisive issue. So together the group thought through who the best speaker would be to address the General Assembly on this topic.

A woman on Bart's committee, Debbie, suggested that they invite Mother Teresa to speak. Bart later admitted the

idea sounded crazy, but he didn't want to squash the creativity.
Mother Teresa had just been awarded the Nobel Peace Prize
and was possibly the most famous woman on Earth. Yet the
committee, wishing to be supportive, reacted positively to the
suggestion.

"So how do we get ahold of Mother Teresa?" Bart asked.

Debbie suggested that they pray. The longer the conversation
went on, the more outlandish the idea seemed to Bart. He held
back his sarcasm about "finding Mother Teresa in the Calcutta
White Pages" (this was obviously pre-Google). At the end of the
meeting, they all decided to pray that they could reach Mother
Teresa.

About six weeks later, Bart received a phone call from Tim,
one of the committee members.

"You won't believe what just happened, Bart," Tim declared.

Then Tim explained to Bart that he had just been at a
conference where he met a Catholic priest by a telephone booth
as they waited to place a call. The two struck up a conversation,
and Tim ended up explaining what his committee was up to.
The priest asked question after question.

Taken aback, Tim finally asked the man why he was so
interested.

"Well, my bishop called last week and told me that I would
be in charge of Mother Teresa's itinerary when she is in the
United States," he said.

So the priest gave Mother Teresa's phone number to Tim,
who gave it to Bart. He made the call, and soon was in dialogue
with Mother Teresa's right-hand nun, Sister Frederick.

"The General Assembly meets for ten days, from June 1
to 10 in St. Louis, so she could come any of those days," Bart
explained to the nun.

"Oh, that's wonderful," Sister Frederick replied.

"Well, do you know which day she'd like to come?" Bart asked.

"Oh, any day would be fine," said the scheduler of the most famous saint on Earth.

"So . . . should I pick a day?" ventured Bart.

"That would be fine," came the reply once more.

"Okay, let's do the fifth."

Again, Sister Frederick was agreeable. "Okay, fine," she said.

"So she'll be there on the fifth?" Bart confirmed in disbelief of the flexibility of Mother Teresa's calendar.

"Oh, I don't know," said the Sister matter-of-factly.

"Okay, I get it, but do you know when you'll know that she'll be there on that day?" Bart asked.

"I don't know."

Bart was baffled. Trying a different approach, he asked the nun where Mother Teresa would be beforehand, and how they could get her to St. Louis.

"Well, I don't know where she'll be but by plane is fine. Or any way."

"When do you know where she'll be beforehand?"

"I don't know when I'll know." The telephone line went silent.

"Bart, I know this is very hard for you," Sister Frederick said, trying to console him. "Mother Teresa is led by the Holy Spirit. If she's driving to the airport and sees a poor person on the side of the road and the Holy Spirit moves her, she will pull over. She will stop the car. And she will help that person."

"But she'd miss her flight!" Bart blurted the obvious.

"I know this is hard for you," soothed Sister Frederick again.

Resigned to the mystery of Mother Teresa, Bart proceeded with the plans of renting the hotel and gearing up for the unknown. Miraculously, Mother Teresa showed up at the 1988 General Assembly to give her remarks.

One of her most remarkable points was this: "If you don't want to love those babies, please send them to me. I will love them."

I don't refer to this episode to try to make a case for or against abortion (although I do have an opinion) but rather to point out what can happen when a few people believe and invest in a vision.

> **To the world, seeing is believing. To Jesus, believing is seeing.**

To the world, seeing is believing. To Jesus, believing is seeing. I heard it said that "faith is when you see ahead of time what makes sense only in reverse." I can't help but think that Bart and his visionary friends knew that they would be a part of history.

Have a Vision

The Greek word *ekthambos* can best be translated as "astounded" or "amazed." It is first used in regard to Jesus when He addressed the Roman centurion who had sent for Jesus to come to his home and heal his servant (Matt. 8:10).

Before Jesus had even reached the sick man, the centurion came outside to greet Jesus. He explained he was a commander of soldiers who obeyed him, and he knew Jesus was a leader whom people and spirits obeyed.

The soldier told Jesus his home was not worthy of the Lord's presence, and he believed Jesus only had to say the word (from outside), and the servant would be healed. Jesus responded: "Truly, I tell you, with no one in Israel have I found such faith."

Jesus was clearly amazed at the centurion's conviction, though it's difficult to imagine Jesus ever being caught off guard.

The other place where Jesus is *ekthambos* is found in Mark 6. It's a scene where Jesus is back in His hometown. All of His family and friends doubted Jesus and His divinity. Mark's account says that Jesus "*marveled* because of their unbelief" and couldn't perform any miracles there.

We most likely find it astounding that Jesus *could do no miracles* because His observers refused to believe. Couldn't the great Creator do anything He wished? Or did He limit Himself because of their display of doubt?

Perhaps this is a glimpse into what Jesus was talking about when He said that the work is to believe. Jesus holds back when those around Him refuse to believe. He seems to count on those who love Him, so He asks us to believe in Him.

Human work and accomplishment find their role front and center in our thinking. King Solomon wrote, "And I saw that all toil and all achievement spring from one person's envy of another. This too is meaningless, a chasing after the wind" (Eccl. 4:4, NIV).

Really!?

All labor and achievement spring from envy!? And it is vanity, a chasing after the wind? We're taught that hard work will move us forward, that it has lasting meaning. We wrongly believe that our work defines us.

Jesus tends to be much more concerned about the invisible, about believing, about dabbling in the world of the unseen. So let's think about faith for a moment.

Faith is really not difficult at all. Every day, we place our faith in chairs, in cars, in planes, in teachers, in GPS, in Wikipedia, and so much more. We have no problem placing our faith in visible things, the tangible things around us: things that we can hear, see, touch, smell, and taste.

It takes another level to believe in the things that we cannot see. And lest we forget, these are the things that last forever. (2 Cor. 4:18)

"Where there is no vision, the people perish," Solomon wrote (Pro. 29:18, KJV).

I've been thinking about vision. I was in Denver once and marveled at the Catholic Basilica there.

Someone had a vision.

My father and I attended Westminster Presbyterian Church, whose architecture to me was unrivaled. Someone had a vision. This year at an international student gathering, we heard a recording of Martin Luther King's "I Have a Dream" speech. Talk about vision—Martin Luther King Jr. owned it.

Jesus had His own vision for twelve disciples. He took rejects and losers and turned them into a force that would redefine history. Our years are numbered by their relationship to Jesus' birth. Shouldn't we take a few measly minutes to study His thoughts?

The Scriptures tell us that faith is "the assurance of things hoped for, the conviction of things not seen" (Heb. 11:1). Paul exhorts us to live by faith, not by sight. James reminds us that faith without works is dead. So how does a person develop faith?

Faith can be a gift extended by God to help us see where we can't. It also has something to do with history. The Jewish festivals and feasts remind them of the great faithfulness of God. Indeed, in remembering, we often find the faith to proceed. More so, I think we develop faith in God the same way we develop faith in a friend. In the beginning, there's a certain degree of simple trust. Then, over time, we come to believe in others despite their failures. So faith is developed over time. As Jesus tells us, faith the size of a mustard seed can move mountains. Part of our faith clearly depends on the depth of our trust. Don't we all yearn for such faith?

Finding Purpose

Golf clubs were not created to be wrapped around trees.

Umbrellas were not meant for beating someone over the head.

Social media was not intended to demean another human.

Keys weren't meant to scratch cars.

Cars were not intended to run over people.

Medicines were not meant to assist in suicide.

A mature man strives to understand the purpose of everything. As much as a third-grade boy is tempted to tug on the ponytail of the girl sitting in front of him, we can misunderstand the purpose of things, even though we see their beauty. That ponytail is designed to be admired, not tugged on.

The good Lord has given us an amazingly wide selection of tools. Each tool has a purpose, and when used for that purpose, it is good. Beautiful things come from tools used for the right purposes. Ugly things result from a perverted use of our tools. With all that we have in our hands, why would we not use each tool in a way that has a positive consequence?

We could use our lawn mower to mow the neighbor's yard. Any good carpenter can turn to his tools to build beautiful additions onto houses. When we share our relationships, we double the joy. Reading an uplifting book brings encouragement.

Each one of us was created with a purpose in mind. When God created Adam, He yearned for companionship. We can see from Jesus' teachings that God desires deeply that we realize His unique love for every person. Most of us will spend our lifetime trying to get our brain around the fact that somehow God loves our pathetic selves.

When we think about why God could possibly love us, we might try to convince ourselves that God needs our help. But He doesn't need us. He enjoys doing things with us, for the connection, but He doesn't *need* our help.

Like a small boy trying to help his dad hoe the garden, we usually do more damage than good. A patient father will allow the young boy to help and then come back later and redo things correctly.

It must be the same way for God. He loves doing things with us, but these things require fixing when it's all done.

Viktor Frankl, Austrian neurologist and psychiatrist and renowned Jewish author who endured the Holocaust in the Auschwitz German concentration camp, wrote a book on the meaning of life (*Man's Search for Meaning*, 1946). As it turns out, he didn't really understand the meaning of life until he had absolutely nothing. Even his name was taken away and replaced with a number. All pride had been drained from his existence.

It was there that he realized that he could fall no farther, where he understood that no other material thing could be taken from him. He sensed it in his nakedness. He realized that when we search for success we seldom find it. Our success lies in the invisible realms as we learn that God loves us.

So what does God want from us? Do we think we will succeed when we try to impress him? Will anything we do bring proper validation?

In the Gospel of Luke we read about a story of two sisters. Martha welcomed Jesus into their home and was busy preparing a meal for Him and His disciples. Her sister Mary sat at Jesus' feet listening to His teaching. When Martha complained, Jesus told her that Mary chose the "good portion" or the better thing (Luke 10:38-42). Usually, Jesus just wants our attention. He favored Mary's approach.

THE SECRET TO SUCCESS

- One who seeks success will never succeed.
- One who seeks fulfillment will never be fulfilled.
- One who seeks fame is destined for obscurity.
- One who seeks influence will have none.
- But one who seeks first the kingdom of God—in all its invisibility—will inherit all things.

5

THE SPIRIT

The Spirit of God first imparts love; He next inspires hope, and then gives liberty; and that is about the last thing we have in many of our churches.

—Dwight L. Moody

A great juggler awes the audience by throwing multiple balls through the air, catching bowling pins and blazing batons with superb accuracy, and even tossing knives or chainsaws with perfect precision. The crowd watches in wonder. How can he keep so many balls in the air? How come he never drops the bowling pins? Why doesn't he feel the heat of the blazing baton? Has he ever been cut by a blade?

The Holy Spirit functions much the same. No one has more balls in the air. He:

- Counsels. (John 14:16-17)
- Teaches us and reminds us of everything Jesus said. (John 14:26)

- Convicts the world of guilt. (John 16:8)
- Guides us into truth. (John 16:13)
- Speaks only what He hears and tells us what is yet to come. (John 16:13)
- Takes from what is Jesus' and makes it known to us. (John 16:14)
- Searches all things, even the deep things of God. (1 Cor. 2:10)
- Helps us understand what God has freely given us. (1 Cor. 2:12)
- Lives in us, His temples. (1 Cor. 3:16)
- Fills us. (Eph. 5:18)
- Is a deposit from God, guaranteeing what is to come. (2 Cor. 5:5)
- Leads us, making us sons of God. (Rom. 8:14)
- Testifies with our spirit that we are God's children. (Rom. 8:16)
- Helps us in our weakness and intercedes for us. (Rom. 8:26)
- Testifies about Jesus. (John 15:26)
- Circumcises the heart. (Rom. 2:29)
- Is the seal of our inheritance. (Eph. 1:13-14)

That's a fair bit, but His tasks are multiplied because He is also specifically working in each life personally, deeply, insightfully, patiently, uniquely, and passionately.

There is a power in our hearts about which we know little. In the hustle and bustle of twenty-first-century America, the Spirit is easily ignored. He works softly, aided by solitude. His presence increases as we seek to understand Him. Those who heed Him are caught up in the wonder and delight of this amazing person.

He is clearly the most mystical member of the Trinity— Father, Son and Holy Spirit. To most, He is difficult to understand. Yet when one begins to comprehend the Spirit's constant workings, teaming up with Him creates bold adventures on the dullest of days.

> **The Spirit does not move according to our procedures, formulas, or schedules.**

How many times have you felt a nudge that you should say something to someone or go out of your way to do something out of the ordinary? Have you followed the prompting or brushed it off? Oftentimes, the inklings we get from the Holy Spirit fly in the face of reason, or at the very least efficiency. Western society values a timeline, but the Holy Spirit does not play by those rules. The Spirit does not move according to our procedures, formulas, or schedules.

My friend Bart learned that the hard way when he attempted to schedule Mother Teresa as a speaker for his event.

Mother Teresa would miss her flight, her reservation, or her speaking engagement to follow the prompting of the Holy Spirit. You might be thinking, "Aren't saints supposed to be responsible? How is missing a flight responsible?!" It's hard to imagine a functional world if everyone followed the Spirit that way. Deadlines would not be met. Payroll would not be made. But perhaps the Lord's business, not ours, would be accomplished—in His own time.

A Moment with Billy Graham

When Billy Graham died, I was reminded of a long-ago time when I was on the receiving end of the Spirit's leading. When I was a twenty-year-old college sophomore from Nebraska working as an intern in Washington, DC, I had two of the coolest internship supervisors any man could imagine.

One was twenty-four-year-old Jon. He was tall and as charismatic as any person I have met. The other was Lyston, a fun-loving and crazy thirtysomething Young Life leader from North Carolina.

My dad had just driven me out from Nebraska, and I was going to spend four months in the big city—Washington, DC. When I arrived, things were hopping. Ronald Reagan had just won his first presidential election and moved to DC about the same time.

I spent three weeks with the army of volunteers who planned and hosted an international prayer gathering from their office in Roslyn, Virginia. Every US president has attended the gathering on the first Thursday of February every year since 1952.

The international assembly is really more of a convention than a breakfast. There are typically about forty-five hundred people from more than 100 countries in attendance.

That year Lyston was sending me all over the hotel, running errands as interns do: call this person, deliver this, pick up that, bring the speaker to his next audience. At 10 a.m. the Wednesday before the event, he told me to go to a certain meeting room and sit in on a meeting.

"Don't say anything," he warned. "Sit in the back and observe what's happening." I found the room and made my way to the back corner, as far from the main door as I could go. It wasn't long before I noticed the room was full of church leaders and evangelists.

I recognized Luis Palau, Bill Bright, Charles Colson, US Sen. Harold Hughes, the Rev. Richard Halverson. I would say about thirty gathered for their own annual meeting.

Each person was taking his turn talking about his ministry. There was a five-minute time limit, but no one paid attention. Each person took more time than was allotted, so I assumed that everyone would not be able to share.

Soon I heard commotion coming from the rear entrance. It looked like a mob scene, but I could see the tall Billy Graham in the middle. The other guests clamored for his attention.

Dr. Graham made his way to the podium to give his address. It seemed as though it was his meeting, and I assumed he had invited the guests. His remarks were brief. He told the participants how much he appreciated them coming and offered his help. He pointed out a few persons in attendance and didn't say much more.

The entirety of his remarks could not have taken more than two minutes. When he was done, Billy began to make his way toward the door. He probably had another appointment he needed to attend. The mob surrounded him again.

Then, before I realized what was happening, he turned his head to the back corner of the room. He made a left turn, leaving the group of glad-handers and made a beeline toward me. I didn't know whether to be honored or afraid. Billy Graham walked straight up to me and put out his hand.

"What is your name?" he asked.

"My name is Brad Olsen from Nebraska. Lyston sent me down to observe your meeting."

"So what brings you here?" he asked.

"I am an intern. Jon and Lyston are in charge of my time."

"And have you been learning a lot?" he asked.

About this time, I felt like the most important man in the building. Billy's genuine interest ignited a flame inside me.

"Yes, I'm just getting started, but I'm learning a lot."

Our conversation probably lasted three minutes or less. I'm sure the men in attendance wondered to whom Billy Graham had given his valuable attention. As Billy talked to me, I got the feeling that there was no one else in the world. I'll never forget it.

After a short but intentional conversation, Billy turned and headed back to the mob. He shook a few hands and exited.

Most people will remember Billy Graham for his immense speaking abilities, his worldwide travel, his massive revival gatherings, his relationship with every president of my early lifetime, the books he authored, and the fame that he couldn't avoid.

Others of us will remember him for his spiritual leading, his love of family, and his immense relational skills. And though his health issues kept him from the limelight in his last years, this world will miss him.

I will look forward to seeing him in the next.

The Reality of Angels

One can't help but notice the presence of angels, if we are paying attention. They show up in the creation story. They show up throughout the Old Testament. They beckon the coming of Jesus. They protect, they encourage, they come to us in disguises. Yet we hardly hear about them today.

So what would it look like if we believed that angels were all around us?

The first thing that comes to mind is the instruction from the writer of Hebrews: "Do not neglect to show hospitality to strangers, for thereby some have entertained angels unaware" (Heb. 13:2).

This way of thinking of strangers and hospitality may stretch us as we've never been stretched before. Looking back, is it possible that you have entertained an angel in the last week? Or this morning? Or is it possible that they have been here all along?

Wouldn't it be wise for us to be on the lookout for them? Could it be the person who helps us in some exceptional way and sort of disappears from the scene was an angel? Could it be that when we helped someone we were actually helping an angel?

My wife, Beth, had developed a dreadful fear of flying. That makes sense because she had survived two airplane crashes. Yes, really! That's another story. When I met her, she was still able to fly on airplanes.

When she became a mother, however, the fear of flying gripped her. It probably had something to do with her maternal instincts and not wanting to leave her children behind.

Yet for some reason, seven years later, she had an inkling to fly again. Crazy as it sounds, we picked a flight right into the Bermuda Triangle for her first time back on a plane. As our departure day approached, her anxiety peaked.

We packed up and drove to the airport, parked the car, and went to check in for her first flight in years. Every step for Beth was a giant leap.

When we reached the Delta counter, the man at the desk was most friendly.

We mentioned to him that it was her first flight in years, and she had some anxiety. Later, at the gate, we saw the attendant as we boarded.

As we went to our seats, we noticed the plane was packed and terribly hot. We scrunched ourselves into our two economy seats. As I looked around the plane, I could feel Beth crush my hand with hers.

Turning to look at her, I realized the panic. I took her hand, and we headed for the exit. The attendants were just shutting the door, but we told them there was no way we could stay on the plane. We walked back up the jetway defeated.

Who do you suppose was the first person we found? It was the same kind attendant who helped us check in. He walked us back down, helped us recover our luggage, and told us what our options were with the tickets. We went to a hotel.

We slept a couple hours, then Beth said she wouldn't mind trying it again if we could somehow get first class tickets. It somehow seemed right to spend a fortune buying first class tickets to Bermuda from Omaha the day of the flight.

We felt like we needed a breakthrough.

When we got back to the airport, guess who was at the desk? The same helpful attendant. He helped us exchange our tickets and walked us back up to the gate. We got on the plane and flew safely to Bermuda.

Despite the fact that we often flew out of Omaha and often used Delta, we never saw our friend again. Through the entire process, we referred to him as our "angel". And we believe that he was. We still talk about "him" often, when we feel the need to be emboldened against our fears.

Understanding the Kingdom of God

Perhaps one of the most difficult concepts for us to comprehend is the kingdom of God. The New Testament is littered with the expression, often mentioned by Jesus.

The first thing we must understand about the kingdom of God is that it's difficult to understand. Jesus says so Himself. He said He spoke in parables so people *won't* understand. And clearly His contemporaries were confounded.

Jesus understood how difficult it would be to wrap a human mind around the kingdom of God. So instead of describing exact specifications of the kingdom, He spoke in similes (for those who forgot from high school English, a simile is a comparison that begins with the words *like*—this word is vastly misused by most everyone today—or *as*).

Because Jesus knew that no one would completely understand these complex concepts, He gave illustrations to help us grasp it. He compared the kingdom of God to various things while unveiling its vast importance.

He said, "Let us seek first the kingdom of God and his righteousness, and all these things [worldly needs] will be added to you" (Matt. 6:33). In other words, all the important things in life (Remember? The invisible things?) are found when we seek the kingdom of God.

The kingdom of God is revealed in prayer.

The kingdom of God is revealed in prayer. In Jesus' greatest prayer, we find the expression, "Your kingdom come, Your will be done" (Matt. 6:10).

Think about this kingdom. Though invisible, it is a place where the King reigns, there are citizens, and there is an economy, like in visible kingdoms. The kingdom of God actually has currency, chain of authority, battles, and schedules too.

Nicodemus, a member of the Jewish Sanhedrin, visited Jesus at night to discuss His teachings. Jesus told Nicodemus that he actually needed to be reborn to enter the kingdom of God. Jesus confused the poor soul, who was fixed in his pharisaic ways.

"How can a man be born when he is old?" Nicodemus asked. "Can he enter a second time into his mother's womb and be born?"

This is confusing when one ponders the biological gymnastics that a physical rebirth would require. Thus, if we want to fathom the infinite kingdom of God, we must completely put off the old thoughts and invite new ones in. We must be born into a new, spiritual family into which Jesus ushers us. Paul said our mind needs to be changed each day (Rom. 12:2).

Jesus said that the kingdom of God was "at hand" (Mark 1:15). What does that mean? If it is at hand, it is close. It is right next to us, yet we can't see, hear, feel, or touch it. One gets the feeling that it's right there, with a thin veil dividing our world and the next.

The writer of Hebrews mentions that we have "a cloud of witnesses" watching all that we do (Heb. 12:1-2). Have you ever thought that you lived your life in an arena with millions looking on? To consider this is to embrace the weightiness of the kingdom of God.

To enter God's kingdom, we must allow for mystery. Authors have tried to capture this sense. C. S. Lewis described his version of it in his book *The Last Battle*. The great dividing line between life in this world and the next, for Lewis, was a stable door. Coming out the other side, the children were reacquainted with fellow adventurers from the annals of Narnia history.

St. Augustine wrote about the City of God and the City of Man. He thought exhaustively about what it would mean to truly understand the City of God, an invisible world ordered by God himself. Dallas Willard wrote *The Divine Conspiracy* to try to grasp the idea of the kingdom.

The kingdom of God is highlighted in Jesus' Sermon on the Mount, which some have dubbed his coronation address. Jesus presents simile after simile about the kingdom of God.

Somehow, He believed it to be formative to the lives of His followers. Oftentimes His messages would be so harsh that thousands would walk away. Yet He never turned from his ideas. Here is a sampling of Jesus' teachings:

-- The kingdom of God is like a good wheat field into which weeds were sown. (Matthew 13:24)

-- The kingdom of God is like a mustard seed, and with a faith that size one can move mountains. (Matthew 13:31)

-- The kingdom of God is like leaven, which is invisible, but it causes the whole loaf of bread to rise. (Mathew 13:33)

-- It is like a hidden treasure. (Matthew 13:44)

-- It is like finding the pearl of great price. (Matthew 13:45)

-- It's like a dragnet. (Matthew 13:47)

-- The wicked will not inherit the kingdom of God. (1 Cor. 6:9)

-- It's like workers in a vineyard. (Matthew 20:1)

-- It's like a wedding banquet, with invited guests. (Matthew 22:2)

-- He tells us who is greatest in the kingdom of God. (Matthew 18:3)

-- The Beatitudes are filled with references to it too. (Matthew 5:2-12)

The above are just a sampling. Look up each reference. You will find a rich treasure at the end of each search.

One of the keys to entering the kingdom of heaven is repentance. John the Baptist's motto was, "Repent for the kingdom of heaven is at hand." Somehow our repentance is tied to heaven.

Oswald Chambers captures the importance of repentance to the kingdom in his book *My Utmost for His Highest:*

> The entrance into the kingdom is through the pangs of repentance crashing into a man's respectable goodness; then the Holy Ghost, who produces these agonies, begins the formation of the Son of God in the life.

> The new life will manifest itself in conscious repentance and unconscious holiness. Never the other way about. The bedrock of Christianity is repentance. Strictly speaking, a man cannot repent when he chooses; repentance is a gift of God.

> If ever you cease to know the virtue of repentance, you are in darkness. Examine yourself and see if you have forgotten how to be sorry.[4]

Here's something Jesus gives us to chew on: The least in the kingdom of God is better than John the Baptist. John, remember, was considered by Jesus to be the greatest man born of a woman (Matt. 11:11).

The conflux of these two ideas might leave us bewildered. Let's get this right: John was the greatest man ever born of a woman, yet in the kingdom of God, the least is greater than John. Clearly Jesus must do some incredible work to alter the sinful soul in order to make it greater than John the Baptist himself. It's hard to imagine a more upside-down thought.

The Kingdom in New York City?

How does a person learn about the kingdom of God?

This is a question we weighed for years in regard to creating real-life experiences for our interns. In 2006, our friend George came up with the following idea: "What if we send the interns two by two to New York City with no money? We would ask them to find out what God was doing and to become a part of it."

Obviously, such a mission could take on many faces, but the bottom line would be an absolute dependence on God to provide food, shelter, friends, significant work, and in some years, protection from the freezing temperatures.

George based his idea on something that Jesus did with His own disciples. Jesus sent them, two by two, to visit surrounding villages. Most of their instructions had to do with what not to bring.

"Carry no moneybag, no knapsack, no sandals, and greet no one on the road" (Luke 10:4). He also told them that they should go out among the Jewish people and bring a peace upon their homes. If they were turned away, they should shake the dust off their feet and move on.

When we read the account upon the disciples' return, we can't help but feel their excitement: "The seventy-two returned with joy, saying, 'Lord, even the demons are subject to us in your name!' " (Luke 10:17).

What Jesus and His disciples proved was that they could depend on God, and when they saw God respond, it stirred their spirits.

We found the same to be true of our male interns. We decided to go ahead with the experiment. Each group was given a credit card and a cell phone for emergencies and told to check in daily. And wow, did we ever pray for them while they were away!

Not only did they find themselves in the midst of excitement and adventure, but they also came back with a newfound enthusiasm about their faith and the way that God had wondrously met their every need.

We have been doing the same every year since. (These trips normally took place in late February or March, and one year our young men had to brave a blizzard.) In practically every case they were amazed at God's provision and presence in their lives.

When I think about the kingdom of God, I can't help but think about these young men. In each group of two (just as Jesus sent His disciples out in twos), young men were emboldened to trust their God for things that no random incident could provide.

Once again, as Jesus said, the kingdom of God is at hand, even as our young men walked the streets of New York City.

Before we sent them into New York, we had sensitized them to recognize the kingdom of God around them. I think most of us are pretty weak on this today. We are so distracted that we seldom see how God is invisibly at work around us.

Indeed, God is all around us, working His ways in people whom we seldom recognize. If we really want to be in tune with God and His mysterious dealings, we simply must learn the art of recognizing God, His works, His people and His kingdom.

6

PERSPECTIVE

"Buying more books than one can read is nothing less than the soul reaching toward infinity."

—*A. Edward Newton*

Let's consider a timeline that instead of having a beginning and an end, has an arrow at each end. Then, if we pick any point on the timeline, no matter how far it is from the left or right, it will remain the same distance from its ending point (which obviously doesn't exist).

This is how our mind struggles with the idea of infinity. It is no wonder that the ancients used a figure eight on its side as its symbol (∞). The symbol represents a path with no end. As any item moves in either direction, it can go as far as it likes without an end.

So too, when we consider eternity, we can see no end. We can subtract any lapse in time for any activity, and there will still remain an eternity. How can this be? We can subtract any number from infinity, and we are still stuck with infinity.

We are finite. It's a challenge to try to grasp either of these concepts: eternity or infinity. We know they exist, but we cannot prove them. What we do here on Earth means almost nothing compared to our lives in eternity, or the infinite number of years that our soul will experience. No matter what we do or how long it takes, it won't affect the balance of time.

Solomon wrote:

I've seen the business that God has given to the children of man to be busy with. He has made everything beautiful in its time and, He has put eternity into man's heart, yet so that he cannot find out what God has done from the beginning to the end. I perceived that there is nothing better for them than to be joyful and to do good as long as they live. (Ecclesiastes 3:10-12)

It seems from this bit of literary wisdom that God has given us time to learn the things that are important: the invisible things, the things that will last, the things that He wants us to embrace. There truly is "nothing better for them than to be joyful and to do good as long as they live."

God Before . . .

God is nothing if He is not God.

We don't discuss idolatry much these days. Yet it was a dominant issue for early Jews. Idolatry is putting anything before God. We hear about God being a jealous God and might wonder how He can be jealous if we are told not to covet.

When we covet, we are desiring something that is not rightly ours in the first place. When the Bible says God is jealous, it is saying that he is vigilantly guarding what is His rightful possession.

Idolatry is putting anything before God.

It is OK for God to be jealous because He is God, and all things belong to Him. He created everything. Humans can marvel at the miracles they see each and every day. How does a leaf know when to grow?

How does a child know when he or she is hungry? How do our bodies function for close to a full century? How can our minds be so advanced that we can carry on sophisticated conversation for hours on end?

Our capabilities are all products of God's brilliant creative designs. They were no accident or the result of some random eruption (unless of course, creation *was* the eruption).

Some people, places, or things clearly climb our totem pole of values, and before we know it, we find they are far too high—indeed, perhaps even higher than God. Though idolatry might have become an afterthought to us, we should know it does not take a backseat in God's world.

We are tempted to put any number of things before God, yet the big three are ourselves, other people, and our possessions.

God Before Self

How does self, or the id as Freud referred to it, become so important to us?

In our social-media-crazed culture, narcissism is at an all-time high. Americans don't have to look far to see people who are obsessed with their appearances and go to great lengths to garner "likes" from those who stalk the internet.

Yet Jesus stands in the face of this mentality, reminding us that when we build ourselves up, we set ourselves up for a great fall.

Indeed, the apostle Paul teaches that we need to figure out how to become a "living sacrifice" (Rom. 12:1). Of course, the biggest problem with a living sacrifice is that it can crawl off the altar. How do we position ourselves in such a way that we are able to restrain ourselves and live, decision by decision, for God?

Jesus has an idea. "Whoever finds his life will lose it, and whoever loses his life for [Jesus'] sake will find it" (Matt. 10:39). If you live for Jesus, you find your authentic self.

My golf pro friend Mike discovered Jesus in midlife. He was gifted at golf and gifted with people. He was well aware of this, and his ego followed suit.

After he discovered Jesus, though, his mantra changed. When I visited him after he found Jesus, I noticed a sign above his bag room door: "Anything. For anyone. At any time."

Mike had discovered that he and his staff were at their best when they were meeting the needs of others. To this day, I have seen no other head golf pros waiting at the curb for members, ready to remove clubs from cars, place them on golf carts, and usher them to the golf range.

Needless to say, within a couple years, Mike plucked one of the most coveted golf pro jobs in the region, at the aptly named Happy Hollow Country Club in Omaha. He has carried this servant attitude through the years, and the members love him.

I find Mike to be one of the greatest examples of what it means for a person to lose his life in order to find his life.

Paul wrote:

> If then you have been raised with Christ, seek the things above where Christ is seated at the right hand of God. Set your mind on the things that are above, not on things that are on earth. For you have died, and your life is hidden with God in Christ. When Christ who is your life appears, then you will also appear with him in glory.
> (Colossians 3:1-4)

Mike's journey is a universal pattern of human nature: the loss of self, or ego, in order to gain our true God-given identity. Dante Alighieri's *Divine Comedy*, the work credited with kick-starting the Renaissance, establishes that same pattern.

After losing his way in the woods, Dante treks through circles of hell in his quest to reach heaven. While most high school English classes focus on the grotesque account of the time spent in hell, called the inferno, Dante's journey is much longer, extending through *purgatorio* (purgatory) to *paradiso* (heaven).

At each level of the inferno, Dante witnesses a different horror inflicted on the inhabitants according to their degree of selfishness on Earth. Shaken, he finds himself at the door of purgatory, facing the seven levels he must ascend by repenting for his sins.

At each level he is forgiven and sanctified, reaching a few inches closer to heaven and the mind of God, and away from the fate of hell. He observes that the closer souls get to God, the more they lose themselves to Him.

Yet the ones closest to God do not cease to be, but rather seem to actualize their true selves and their individuality. Dante realizes that, paradoxically, souls gain themselves by giving of themselves.

Mike and Dante were struck by similar epiphanies centuries apart from each other and centuries after Jesus explained "He who loses his life for my sake, will find it" (Matt. 10:39).

Relinquishing the steering wheel to drive in the right direction remains a paradox. It's just one of the ways Jesus turned humanity upside down. When He placed God before Himself, His example echoed throughout the ages, reaching not just a medieval poet in Italy but a twenty-first-century golf pro in Nebraska.

So where does our authentic self actually abide? According to Paul, our real self, the true person who we were designed to be, resides with Jesus in the heavenly place. And it is only by focusing on this divine perspective that we find the "authentic me."

The authentic me is a giver.

One can divide people in the world into two groups: the net givers and the net takers. Which one are you? If we developed the balance sheet of all that you have given versus all you have taken, would you come out in the black?

Most likely someone came to your mind as you processed the idea of the net giver. This person shows sensitivity to the needs of others. And he or she does something about it.

I find that net givers tune themselves to the art of giving. They discover what it is like to reduce the self in order to bless others. It is incumbent upon us to figure out how to dethrone the almighty self. When we do, when we put Jesus on that throne, we find our true position in life. Then we are free to live as God desires.

God Before Others

At the beginning of the chapter I mentioned how the jealousy of God is not the petty third-grade variety but a fierce guarding of His own possession. He created us to connect with Himself. Throughout the Old Testament, we see God's jealousy again and again.

It seems He really wants to be our God. Our only God.

He wants to walk with us, talk with us, relate to us, and fellowship on a deep level.

God tested Abraham's faithfulness when He asked the father to kill his long-awaited promised son. We all know the ending to that story. God inserted himself and stopped Abraham from killing Isaac by providing another sacrifice. So what does Isaac represent? Sure, He represents the promised progeny God gave Abraham. But He also represents something that Abraham could withhold from God. Abraham could actually idolize Isaac by putting Him in the position reserved for God. He tested Abraham, and Abraham passed.

So how does this apply to God and others?

Admittedly, I am a people pleaser. I often put men before God. I love the praise that comes from others, even when it's patronizing. My friend Linda said it best: "I don't care if you have to lie to me. Just give me a compliment."

> **The praise of others can create a brick in the wall between us and our Maker.**

We do love the praise of others, and sometimes that can create a brick in the wall between us and our Maker.

Jerry once went to his local college president. He offered to fund a new program that would target members who hold a C average. "A students" were forbidden from joining. His hypothesis was that over time, the C-caliber mavericks would become better leaders than students who adhered to the status quo and pleased their teachers and parents.

The experiment proved a success. These mavericks didn't really care what others thought about them. They wanted to do what was right. They had a vision, albeit slightly different from the administration's, yet the group became an asset to the college.

How We Should Hate

Jesus says one must hate his or her family in order to follow Jesus.

I have not heard too many sermons on this topic.

Does Jesus really want us to hate the individual members of our family?

This passage is often misunderstood. What Jesus was really saying was that, by comparison, He wants His followers to love Him more than their individual family members.

Jesus says,

> "whoever denies me before men, I also will deny before my Father who is in heaven. Do not think that I have come to bring peace to the earth? I have not come to bring peace, but a sword. For I have come to set a man against his father, and a daughter against her mother, and a daughter-in-law against her mother-in-law. And a person's enemies will be those of his own household. Whoever loves father or

mother more than me is not worthy of me, and whoever loves son or daughter more than me is not worthy of me." (Matthew 10:33-37)

Jesus expects nothing but our best love for Him. Perhaps one of the greatest examples of a Bible figure who cared too much about others' opinion is Peter—in his three denials. After his third time denying Jesus, Peter realized his error. He must have felt demoralized. Once again, Jesus came back to rescue His friend Peter:

> Simon, son of John, do you love me more than these?" He said to him, "Yes, Lord; you know that I love you." He said to him, "Feed my lambs." He said to him a second time, "Simon, son of John, do you love me?" He said to him, "Yes, Lord; you know that I love you." He said to him, "Tend my sheep." He said to him the third time, "Simon, son of John, do you love me?" Peter was grieved because he said to him the third time, "Do you love me?" and he said to him, "Lord, you know everything; you know that I love you." Jesus said to him, "Feed my sheep. (John 21:15-17)

In thus questioning and redeeming Peter three times, Jesus reinstates Peter as His lead disciple.

So once again, Jesus gives His beloved the chance to repent and be reinstated to his former position. In the same way, Jesus forgives us when we care too much about pleasing others.

God Before Possessions

King David writes in Psalm 24,

"The earth is the LORD's and the fullness thereof,
the world and those who dwell therein,
for he has founded it upon the seas
and established it upon the rivers." (Ps. 24:1-2 KJV)

So who do you think owns everything?

Lost in the modern translations of Psalm 24 is the poetry that existed in its original Hebrew. But the message is clear: Everything belongs to God, and when we seek Him, we find His face.

So if God is the owner, who are we? If God is owner, we become His stewards. We become the managers, the chief operating officers, so to speak.

Do we treat our possessions like they belong to someone else? Or do we hoard them and keep them to ourselves? Clearly the owner of our stuff wants us to use it to bless others.

Jesus makes it clear that we should use our resources to help others, even a Samaritan, a religious half-breed rejected by both Jews and Gentiles.

In one of His most powerful stories, Jesus places a man on a lonely road. He had been beaten by criminals. Whereas other religious figures simply walked by, the Good Samaritan not only revived and rescued the man, he provided shelter and food for the next day. He was a hero in the truest sense of the word.

Jesus uses this parable to answer the question, Who is my neighbor? He requires that we love our neighbor in a way that costs something. He is more concerned about the heart of the giver than the response of the receiver.

We may be hesitant to give so much of our resources to help others because we want to make sure we have enough for a rainy day. We want to feel secure. We are constantly trying to build "bigger barns" so that we can store up things to make us independent. Our human desire is to be self-sufficient, so that we do not have to trust God for daily provision.

But He makes it clear that He will provide all that we need.

My friend Steve came to me with a problem. He looked gloomy. He was fretted about the future of his job and wondered aloud how he could ever pay the bills without his salary.

Steve is a dutiful husband and father and takes his responsibilities seriously.

I found myself asking him a rather stern question: "Who ever told you it was your job to provide for your family?"

Steve looked at me like I was from Mars.

"That's what we're supposed to do, aren't we?" he asked.

In the hour that followed we talked about one particular name for God: Jehovah Jireh, the Lord God Provider (Genesis 22:14). God not only provides for us, but His character is embedded in His name.

God loves His children, and He provides.

I don't say that flippantly. I realize people struggle with not having enough. These struggles are painful, and real. So when we don't have enough, what are we to do? We are to pray; we are to trust; we are to seek out the King who owns "the cattle on a thousand hills". (Ps. 50:10) And somehow He shows us how to care for His children.

So what are we to do for those who lack? The Scriptures don't let us just pat the hungry person on the head and send him away with a prayer. We are to do what we can. Yet even with our care, he says there will still be those who don't have enough. We see images of starving children on TV. I honestly don't understand how God lets this happen, or more precisely, how we let this happen. (This is one of the mysteries we discussed earlier.)

So we pray, we believe, and we trust. We should hold God's feet to the fire. If He says that He is, by nature, the Lord God Provider, we should beg Him to provide. Then we need to cultivate what He gives.

Beyond that, I don't have many good answers. But I know God takes great pleasure in us when we take care of our fellow man.

So back to my friend Steve. By the end of our conversation, Steve decided it would be better for him to pray and believe than to worry and fret. He began to do so. He kept his job, and the Lord has provided for his family.

Jesus as the Word

The message is a person!

> He visited Abraham: "After these things, the word of the LORD came to Abraham in a vision. 'Fear not, Abraham, I am your shield, your reward shall be very great.' " (Gen. 15.1)

> He visited Moses. "So Moses listed them according to the word of the LORD, as he was commanded." (Num. 3:16)

> He visited Samuel: "Now Samuel did not yet know the Lord, and the word of the LORD had not yet been revealed to him." (1 Sam. 3:7)

He visited Nathan: "That night, the word of the LORD came to Nathan, saying. . ." (2 Sam. 7:4)

He visited David, and his seer Gad: "And when David arose in the morning, the word of the LORD came to the prophet Gad, David's seer. . ." (2 Sam. 24:11)

He visited Solomon: "The Word of the Lord came to Solomon." (1 Kings 6:11)

We could cite dozens more examples of how the word of the Lord came to prophets and kings in the Old Testament. But Who is the Word? For years, my evangelical friends referred to their Bible as "The Word."

It made sense to me. It is inspired by God. And typically, the words belong in the literary realm where, strung together, they comprise sentences, chapters, and books. Imagine the surprise when I discovered that the Word was a person, a person about whom we've heard plenty.

Indeed, God wrapped His message around His only Son, whom He sent to Earth as a human being. But before that, this person, the Word, visited a host of heroes of the Old Testament. In fact, the Word has been present since the dawn of creation, according to the apostle John.

If I were a Jew familiar with the Old Testament, all the alarm bells and whistles on my mental dashboard would go crazy when I read what John wrote: "In the beginning was the Word and the Word was with God, and the Word was God. He was in the beginning with God . . . and the Word became flesh and dwelt among us" (John 1:1-2, 14).

To any Jew, with all the connections to the Word of the Old Testament, this would have been profound. All things were created through this so-called Word of God.

This begs the question, did creation or did words come first? Genesis is clear that God spoke the universe into creation. He spoke a word and creation appeared. Over and over.

How are the heavens made? "The heavens were made by the breath of his mouth" (Ps. 33:6).

So now we find Jesus in the very beginning of creation, throughout the Old Testament as the Word of the Lord, and made flesh in the Gospels. He walked planet Earth and taught a myriad of lessons, many of which were recorded by His disciples.

If God deals in messages, we should ask ourselves, "How good is God at communicating?"

Well, let's detail some of the ways that He communicates with us:

- Through the Word, His son Jesus, and all of His teachings.
- Through creation and all the ways that God communicates to us through it.
- Through the Holy Spirit, the Teacher, who lives inside every believer.
- Through other people.
- Through millions of experiences over the course of a lifetime.
- Through family and the experiences therein.
- Through writings and teachings.
- Through various roles we play over the course of a lifetime.

- In dreams, which can sometimes be vibrant, emotional, and personal.
- In a myriad of other unique and creative ways.

In a way, God is constantly sending us signals and communications. He's constantly teaching us various truths about life, not the least of which would be the height and width and depth and breadth of His great love for us. In fact, He would be satisfied if we simply would embrace His love for us.

Yet God went one step farther by creating our capacity for awareness of Him. God promises, "I will put my law in their minds, and write them on their hearts" (Heb. 8:10).

How can anything be more personal than that? God Himself writes His law in our minds and on our hearts and walks with us as the Word of the Lord did with the heroes of old.

So then what role does the Bible play? Well, the Bible is the Scriptures. The word *Bible* never appears. Paul writes, "All Scripture is breathed out by God and profitable for teaching, for reproof, for correction, and for training in righteousness, that the man of God may be complete, equipped for every good work" (2 Timothy 3:16-17).

If we want a manual for life, we need look no farther than the Scriptures, which were inspired by God and profitable for every important thing that we do on Earth.

I would say that God is pretty good at communicating. He engages every sense. He reminds us every minute. He gets right down to the minutia. His messages never cease. They permeate us every moment.

The Scriptures, and indeed Jesus Himself, help equip us to hear Him clearly. Solitude helps. The Holy Spirit translates and teaches.

Jesus regularly went away from His disciples to refocus, to pray, and to engage the Father. For centuries, Jews have taught their children to memorize the Scriptures. In this way, we can actually carry God's inspired words with us, creating a file cabinet of topics that the Holy Spirit can access at any moment.

So, at any time, in any way, engaging any sense, and enduring forever, the Lord sends us His message. And we choose whether or not to receive it.

7

THE INNER RING

Brothers on mission forming small radiants of light are bearers of Christ simply by their presence. Without knowing how, through this simple Christ-like presence, God assures and transfigures this world slow to believe.

—Rule of Taize

Life sometimes seems like a game.

Much like Monopoly, in real life a person moves around a three-dimensional board, gathering houses, a salary, pays doctors' fees, cashes out bonds, and hopefully never goes directly to jail.

In our youth, my friends and I believed that when we died, and this mystical board game (life) was complete, the winner would be the one with the most money. Later in life, I watched one person after another chase after the almighty dollar. They bought into the notion that a man was created to simply pursue money. That pursuit ended badly.

I thought that, as an aspiring dentist (I never became one), I could make the money of a doctor without having to work crazy hours. As it turned out, when I actually visited an office and watched, the process was frustrating, repetitive, exacting, and painful for the patient.

I found that I really didn't like the idea of exacting pain on people. (No offense intended to dentists.)

Fortunately, some deeper friends came along later in high school and college. They challenged me to embrace a quite different currency: friendship. The closer I got to these friends, the more I realized that they *did* relationships better than anyone I'd met before.

I was sucked in. Fast-forward to today, my wife and my children have built networks of friends by using the things we saw others model.

The famous philosopher and theologian C. S. Lewis wrote an address called the Inner Ring that brilliantly describes a common state of the human soul. In it he hypothesizes that every person yearns for significant relationships.

We all journey through life, jumping from one friend group to the next: a preschool class, the neighborhood kids, a baseball team, a dance troupe, a football team, a fraternity or sorority at college, a certain work group in one's career, a church, or any number of other groups.

The fact of the matter is, we wander through life bouncing from one group to the next hoping to discover relational nirvana. Once we find a circle of authentic friends, we strive to get inside.

It seems as if those inside are living life to its fullest. Yet we sit on the outside yearning to be in. We spend time, money, energy, emotions, and our belongings trying to get inside this circle. For those of us fortunate enough to reach the inside, we realize two things:

1. The inner circle is not as appealing on the inside as it looks from the outside, and

2. We discover another ring within the ring and start all over again to work ourselves in.

Clearly something within us yearns for authentic friendships. These friendships prove to be gratifying, but they also prove to be painful or difficult. Then we must learn to do the required maintenance on our friendships.

Maintaining the relationship requires us to humble ourselves, to defer to another's way, to say we're sorry when we do something wrong, to place the others' needs ahead of our own. Yet, in the end, these bonds draw us to heavenly things. So in the end money isn't everything.

Something within us yearns for authentic friendships.

The website *Business Insider* conducted a study in 2016 of winners of major lotteries and discovered that winning the Powerball lottery did not make the winners happier. In fact, many of the winners found themselves friendless or penniless or both.

Instead, those who grow old collecting friends experience the opposite. They feel surrounded by love and that they have enough even when financially they might be lacking. Their lives have significance and meaning.

Years ago I met regularly with three other men to share our spiritual lives. Because we found it virtually impossible to agree on a reasonable time and place for us to meet we settled for an unreasonable time: 6 a.m. on Friday mornings at a place that was about a forty-five-minute drive for me. Ouch.

This was a vital, though bleary-eyed, time of fellowship for me. The conversation ultimately always landed on some deep, important, and personal topic that we were not discussing with other people. This group became a support to us. We rarely missed a Friday meeting.

The first time we met, we asked for a private table in a room that wasn't open. We carried our Bibles. Mike D, our waiter that day, later told us that none of the wait staff wanted to handle us, so Mike D drew the short straw.

Mike D was a partier, a self-described pothead, a long-haired guy with an intense Baltimore accent. He wore black Converse high top shoes and "dungarees" (most of us refer to them as blue jeans) and loved to be belligerent. His cynicism was caustic. There was generally no good reason for him to like any of us.

Somehow, over the course of months, Mike D grew to like us. When coming to get our order, he would stay and chat for a half hour. He was curious about every topic we were discussing.

We eventually became friends. He introduced me to his then girlfriend of sixteen years, Angie. They both ended up coming to work with me in our family's newspaper company. Mike D and Angie eventually were married, and I attended a small wedding to witness their nuptials.

So why would a guy like that have any interest in four guys with whom he had no common ground? I can't help but believe that it had something to do with Lewis' idea of the Inner Ring.

Somehow this group of four guys, meeting early in the morning on Fridays, appealed to a hippie who was still loaded from last night's party. Mike D would later write the account of these meetings. Allow me to introduce you to him. Here is the story as he tells it. I think you will enjoy it from his vantage point:

I was already on my third cup of coffee and still wasn't sure if I was ready for the day yet, but it was time to take that last drag of my cigarette and last swallow of coffee before the manager of the restaurant opened the front door at 6 a.m. as he did every day. The breakfast rush at that hour was not really a rush at all. I just had to be there for any of those customers who would stop by for a cup of coffee and maybe an order of toast. It was probably still dark outside, but who could tell when you work in a place with no windows? I just remember that it didn't matter what it was like outside because I was obligated to be there until at least 2 p.m., and all I could think about was making some cash to spend at the bar after work. I was waiting tables, which is what I had been doing for a living for quite some time, and working for tips almost guaranteed that I would have cash in my pocket on a daily basis.

Friday always seemed to be the longest day at work. It was the end of the week and the party began at 2 p.m., or just a little thereafter. It was also a day when the more tips you make, the more you can drink at the end of the day. Most seasoned waits can smell what kind of tip they are going to make on a table, and I was one of the best there was at this. Since it was still early morning a few of the waits and I were rotating tables, or we'd pick up the tables when we knew the customer. Mostly we were hanging out grabbing a few puffs of a cigarette or gulps of coffee. If we saw a table we would rush off to grab it or we would push it off on another wait, and sometimes beg some other wait to take care of it. On this morning, I had pushed off all the tables I could possibly hand off, and in walks four men in business suits. First of all, they chose to sit in a section of the restaurant that was closed, and second, suits are not that great of a tip. Besides, when you've been in the business as long as I had been, you know that when a foursome of men in suits want a private area, they either want to have a business meeting or it's a bunch of Jesus Freaks who have come to pray.

Right away the other waits didn't want to wait on these guys, because waiters are beggars and we are only doing this kind of job for the cash. There is certainly no glory at all in this career. I just happened to be the waiter with the slowest section, mainly because I had been pushing my tables off on some other wait, and also because I seemed to be the wait that always got stuck with the tables no other wait wanted. If it were a bunch of ladies who wanted separate checks, I would most assured have that table. If it was a family with a dozen screaming children, that would be my table too. So there I was, stuck waiting on these four guys in business suits.

After they sat down and I gave them a once over, I realized they weren't arrogant enough to be businessmen, so that only left one thing that they could be. My lucky day, four Jesus Freaks, I thought. And this really was something I wasn't ready to deal with at 6 a.m. on a Friday.

When I took their drink order, there wasn't a coffee drinker in the bunch. Three glasses of water and a glass of iced tea. Then and there I knew that I had some major big spenders. After their meal, their total guest check came to about five dollars, which meant even with a 15 percent tip, I wouldn't make enough to buy a pack of rolling papers. I had been working at this restaurant for quite some time and a trained wait remembers people who come and go, usually by the tip they leave or don't leave. This was the first time I had seen these guys, so I figured it was a one-time deal and wouldn't worry about the size of the tip, which I expected to be very small— not that the service was bad, but let's face it, how great a service can one provide on a five dollar check. To my surprise, or should I say shock, the tip wasn't all that bad. It was over two dollars, and waits only have to claim 8 percent of their sales, so I was ahead of the game. I got through the table with very little talk and no introductions and still had enough cash for that pack of papers and a drink at the local bar.

A week went by, and I was trying to wake up again, when they showed up again. They were back at their same table, and I was their waiter once more. Three waters and an iced tea. The challenge was on, I've always loved a challenge, and if any waiter in the house could get a customer to buy more food, to build up a check to make a bigger tip, I was the one to do it. Not only was I one of the highest tipped waits, but I could snag a tip from a non-tipper, or stiff, as they are referred to in the service industry.

There are many ways to build a tip up on a customer, and I was known to do this with many a customer in my day. I was one of the best, and I went in for the kill on this table. When you're dealing with someone who is a sports enthusiast, you give them the scores. If it's a table of ladies, you tell them how great their perfume is. When you're dealing with Jesus Freaks, you got to go for the religion thing.

At the time I was a non-practicing Catholic, which means I knew nothing about religion. I figured I could con these guys or at least fake them out. Pulling a con on someone takes time if it's going to be successful. During my trips to the table to deliver their food or fill their water and one iced tea, I would ask them questions about *what they were doing, nothing major. I would also throw in a few things on me being a Catholic and maybe just check to see how their food was. I really didn't care as long as they left the tip.*

These guys got to the restaurant as soon as the doors opened, and since I'd get high on my way to work so I could get through the morning, I'd usually be stoned when I waited on them. This is what most of the people in the restaurant and bar business did. It was a way of coping with the stress that we have put up with from customers, managers, or fellow waits who didn't know what they were doing. Also, it wasn't like I worked in a situation where I had to be alert.

Drugs and alcohol was a way of life for me and I made no bones about it. Most of my co-workers knew this. They also knew I could function and do my job well under these circumstances. Besides everyone did it. It was basically what our lives were about, go to work, get high, get drunk, sneak in a few hours of sleep, and do it all over again. When your circle of friends do drugs, your connections are tight. If I was to run out of dope, there was always someone I could call for some sort of drug. Whenever the drugs went dry, there was always a bar around where I could get drunk. Living this way is dangerous though. There is always a chance of getting busted for drugs or a DWI or just owing someone a lot of money for something that doesn't last a very long time. Keep this in mind, drugs and alcohol wear off, and the longer you've been using the lower the high and the less time it will be in between a fix. A quick fix is just that. Quick. Then it's over.

With each passing Friday, I knew that these four guys would come in the restaurant. Each time I asked more questions and got more answers. Sometimes I understood what they were saying to me, but for the most part I was so stoned that I really wasn't paying much attention to their answers.

As time went on I got to know those guys a little better and our time on Friday morning got a little more personal. After getting to know their eating habits, the next step was getting to know their names and form opinions of them. At some point I stopped referring to them as Jesus Freaks and started referring to them as my Christian customers.

First of all there was Brad. I pegged him as an intelligent man who had it together and the leader of this little group. He spoke so well, like everything he said I was meant to hear. Believe me, I tried not to because I just wasn't interested in what he was selling, and I wasn't about to buy something I didn't think I needed. The truth was that I couldn't help but listen. It was like this magnet of truth came out with every syllable that he spoke. I really despised him for this because I was used to listening to people who told me what I wanted to hear and not the truth. Brad also had the energy about him. It was electrifying, like seeing the ice cream man on a hot summer day.

Then there was Bart. Bart appeared to be that quiet kid in class who you always wondered what was on his mind. He also seemed to have a heart of gold. He didn't really speak all that much, but when he did, it was always kind and soothing. I could almost picture him sitting under a tree in a field of wildflowers just enjoying the beauty of the world. Bart didn't have to speak to get his message across; he seemed to send out good vibrations by just being there. He was the kind of person who would do the right thing for the right reasons. He was most definitely an intricate part of this little group. Bart was what I might call a brown suit. Most people look drab in a brown suit but put Bart in a colosseum of men in tuxedos and you would certainly know he was there by the love he had for humankind.

Scott intimidated me. A man of his youth shouldn't be so wise. It was like King Solomon wrapped up in Joe College. He not only said wise things, I could also see a wisdom in his eyes. This man was as intense as an old wise owl. Even though we joked now and then, his wisdom was just too much for me to handle. He was serious about everything. I might have expected him to be serious about God, after all he was a Christian, but he was also serious about the issues that were going on in the world. Right was right and wrong was wrong. There didn't seem to be a middle ground on any issue. I enjoy a good healthy argument once in a while, but this was one man I didn't want to tangle with because I knew he would win, and the sad part is that I think that I would have seen it his way in the end. So I knew it would have been pointless for me to try and put my way of thinking up against his. Put it this way, if I was up for a crime in front of a judge, and he was the judge, he would find the perfect punishment to give me for my own good and that's the way it would be. I wouldn't want him to be my parent.

Last, but certainly not least, there was Clarke. He was one of the most outrageous men I had ever met in my entire life. This guy had the courage to wear some pretty ugly ties that would turn Medusa to stone. Clarke was certainly different in this group. He was the oldest of the four, but you would have thought he was the youngest. Everything about him seemed to be cool. He was just someone you wanted to be around, no matter how outrageous you thought he was. He seemed like the life of the party, and even more. He seemed to be what life should be. He was himself without reservation, and he followed God's rules, and he did it so well. It was sometimes hard to listen to him because my eyes were drawn to his tie and my brain was saying to me: "What was he thinking when he bought that tie?" If I'm fortunate enough to meet up with Clarke in heaven, I'm sure I'll recognize him by his paisley print wings.

These four guys formed a special bond, but still there was something I was missing and I wasn't sure what it was at the time. It also seemed that the more I got to know them, the more intrigued I became with this group of different men.

While all this was going on at work, my life outside of work was still one big party—with one exception. I was six months from becoming forty years old, and I wasn't ready for it. I've always thought of myself as a nineteen-year-old hippie, without responsibility, living life to the fullest. Things were pretty good for me at home, I had a girlfriend that I had been living with for over sixteen years. Our relationship was stable, and we were able to pay our bills. I was pretty much happy as far as I knew. My only hang up was turning forty. Turning forty was not going to stop me from being what I always was, and if necessary, I would just lie about my age. I thought that I had settled down quite a bit from the way my life had been five years prior to this. My drug usage had been cut almost in half. The only drug I used on a day-to-day basis was pot. I didn't do much cocaine anymore. Actually the only time I did coke was when it was offered to me, and that wasn't too often. So, I really considered myself pretty clean as far as drugs went. I had been drinking more than ever, but that was legal, so I didn't think too much about that. When you're nineteen years old your body can take more than it could at thirty-nine. What a shock this was to me. But that was alright. I was lying about my age anyway, but in reality I was running scared because the people I was associated with were ten, fifteen, and some twenty years younger than me, and I just couldn't keep up with them like I used to.

Drinking after my shift at work with my fellow waits sometimes kept me out until the bars closed, followed by getting up every morning at 5:30 was just a little more than I could handle at times. Everything seemed to be going against me, my drinking, my drug abuse, and then there was this thirty-nine-year-old body.

One Friday morning my Christian customers were in as usual. I was ready to ask them to start praying for me. I think I just wanted a prayer to get me through the day and nothing more. If I thought their prayers could have changed me into a nineteen-year-old again I would have put that in a written request. I'm just not one to believe in those kinds of miracles.

I could sense our relationship changing at that point, because I wasn't really one to ask someone to pray for me. As time went on these prayers seemed like weekly requests and then something new developed. I no longer thought of these four guys as my Christian customers but as my friends.

I didn't notice it at first, but as each week I found myself spending more time at their table and less time with other customers. I started asking more questions and was starting to listen to their answers.

As each Friday came and went, I expected them to be there. When they weren't there, I was genuinely disappointed and sad that I didn't get the chance to see or talk to them that day. They seemed to have been a bright spot in my day, and I couldn't for the life of me figure out why. There was even a time when I thought that they had gotten tired of that restaurant and moved on to some other meeting place, and that really made me feel bad, because I thought I wouldn't see them again. Well I never thought that way about a customer before, unless they were an extremely good tipper, and believe me that takes a lot.

One night I was at a restaurant bar and ran into Scott and Bart. It just so happened that I wasn't drinking that night because I had given up drinking for a while to give my body a rest from alcohol. Still, I was taken off guard by Scott when he approached me at my usual perch at the bar. I had been smoking a little bit of pot that night, and Scott was the one who intimidated me from the first meeting we had. He started throwing out questions to me about abortion and some pretty serious stuff that I just couldn't handle at that time. I felt like a cornered rat that had no place to run. Scott and Bart asked me to join them for dinner, and I really wanted to but not that night. Marijuana and deep conversation is not a good combination, especially when you're talking with a wise man and a kind man. I would have surely blown my cover, and I wasn't about to risk that. When the two of them went into the dining room to eat, I hit the door faster than a cop in hot pursuit, just in case they came back into the bar after their meal.

The next time I saw them at their Friday morning meeting I was so embarrassed by the whole incident, I tried not to hang around the table that day. When they had left that morning, I felt bad, like I had betrayed a friendship.

Months went by, and the Friday morning meetings continued. All of the other waits knew the table was mine, and heaven help the wait that tried to steal it from me. My fellow waits knew that I was making a good tip from the table, and everyone who worked there was greedy when it came to making a tip, especially an easy one. The tip wasn't so important to me anymore. At that point I wouldn't have cared if they had stiffed me. Just being around those guys gave me a good feeling, even if I wasn't picking up what I was missing. It was something that was going on at that table, there was something that I was really missing. I could almost feel it breathing down the back of my neck. It really bothered me, because I considered myself to have a pretty good keen sense about what was going on around me, but I just couldn't grasp this one.

A few seasons passed and spring was just around the corner. About this time my girlfriend had been given an opportunity to open her own restaurant. She had asked me to quit my job and come help her out. I really didn't want to for two reasons. First of all, we had never worked together before, and I wasn't sure that it would be wise to live with someone and work with them also. More than that, though, I didn't want to leave my job because I knew that I would miss the four guys who seem to be putting my life into a new perspective. Although, it wasn't a great change, I had noticed that something was happening in my life, and it was good. I decided to give my notice to my manager at the restaurant, which wasn't all that hard to do. I also told the guys about this new restaurant that I had decided to go to and more or less pleaded with them to come over and have their meetings there since it wasn't too far from where they were meeting already. To my surprise, they said they would be there.

My girlfriend finally opened her restaurant. Weeks went by, but there was no sign of my friends. It was kind of disappointing and I had thought I had been forgotten. Meanwhile, my girlfriend and I were going through some pretty rough times in our relationship. We were fighting day and night about the restaurant and all the hours she was putting in at work. Her partner and I didn't get along. In fact, we hated each other to the point that if he were to drop dead on the spot, I would have thrown a party and invited everyone I knew. All this was going on in my life, and I was about to turn forty years old. I just wasn't coping well with my life, or anything else that happened to be going on around me. I would leave work every day and head straight for the bar and get extremely drunk. By the time I got home, I was ready for a knockdown, drag out fight, which seemed to be happening daily. In a matter of a few weeks, my

*life had gotten so screwed up that I knew I was going to hit bottom
before I even turned forty.*

*A friend from the restaurant where I used to work came in to
see me. She told me my friends were meeting at a different place for
the past few weeks, that they hadn't been in the restaurant since I
wasn't working there anymore. This made me feel real special. She
also told me that she told my friends that my girlfriend's restaurant
was open. That very next Friday there they were at the door bright
and early at 6 a.m. just like old times. When I saw them a smile
brightened my face, but not half as big as the one in my heart.*

*Friday was the only day I enjoyed being at work. I hated that
restaurant with a passion, mainly because I didn't get along with
my girlfriend's partner, and my co-workers were bringing me down.
Everyone there was making it real tough for me. Anyway, there they
were, Brad, Bart, Scott, and Clarke sitting in a corner booth in
their own section of the restaurant, three glasses of water and a glass
of iced tea. Something else brightened up that corner booth, and
whatever it was I still wasn't getting it.*

*One afternoon when I was about to leave work, Bart called
and invited me to a prayer breakfast. Why not? I thought. What
have I got to lose? Just the idea that I had gotten an invitation made
me feel better than I had in weeks. So I took him up on his offer and
met them for this breakfast. I had no idea what it was all about.*

*When I got to this prayer breakfast, there were about six
hundred people in the room. At first, I didn't know what to think,
but I went in anyway. There was something about this mass of
people in prayer that was kind of comforting, also it also seemed
natural, at least for those six hundred people. Also, everyone seemed
genuinely happy, which to me seemed a little unusual, especially for
the way I had been feeling in the last few weeks. I have to admit,
when I walked out of that room that morning, I felt better myself.*

Forty was less than a month away, and I was getting really scared. So scared I knew I had to get away from everyone and everything that I knew. My girlfriend suggested I go down to Florida to where we spent a few years. I had always liked being in Florida because I was happy when I was there, not only happy, but I spent some of the best years of my life there. So on Memorial Day weekend I drove to Florida to get away from all the turmoil in my life. Actually, I think she wanted me to get away from her for a while because I was driving her insane. She couldn't keep up with her work, and our daily fights that were tearing us apart. She was more than willing to foot the bill, which also told me that she wanted me to go.

Florida wasn't all that I thought it would be, and it was really too much for me to handle without drugs and alcohol. Being down there only made me feel more alone, and I was missing my youth more than ever before. I did some major abuse to myself and then decided it was time to say goodbye to yesterday and give in to middle age.

When I returned home, my girlfriend told me I didn't need to come back to work, and I really wasn't wanted there because I was miserable and also making everyone else's life miserable. So there I was, turning forty, unemployed, and my friends all thought I had gone off my rocker. I had the blues big time. Sitting around the house was like being in a prison to me. I had no ambition to go out and look for a job or even go out for some air. The only thing that was going through my mind was revenge. Revenge was eating me up inside. I thought that getting back at these people for doing this to me would satisfy me, if only for a little while. It was just easier to blame them for my problems than blame myself.

Friday rolled around, and I was thinking about my friends. Actually, I was missing them. They had seemed to be the only bright spot during that time in my life. I asked my girlfriend to ask them to pray for me and give them my phone number. Much to my surprise, the phone rang, and it was Brad. After talking to him, I felt 100 percent better and my spirits were lifted greatly just by the sound of his voice. There also seemed to be this energy all around me that morning. The phone conversation led to an invitation to church with him and his family. At first I was reluctant, but then I thought maybe that's just what I needed. He said he would be in contact. That Friday and Saturday night turned out to be one of the worst weekends of my life and my relationship with my girlfriend. I got crazy drunk, caused a major argument, went home and tore up our apartment and even threw out the cats for the night. It was really out of character for me. I'm the kind of person who usually has control of my life. That night I didn't think I had much of a life at all. I thought I had lost everything. I was sure that my relationship with my girlfriend was over and that I had to make some big decisions. I was now in a major depression. The blues I had been having over the past few weeks seemed like a ride on the merry-go-round.

Sunday morning Brad called just as he promised, and by the sound of my voice he could tell that I had just gone through a bad night. It didn't matter. Nothing was going to keep me from church that morning, not even a blizzard in June. When Brad came to pick me up for church, I'm sure I looked as if I had been beaten and thrown out with the trash. He had his wife and children with him, and when he introduced me to them, I felt as if I was being welcomed like a long-lost member of the family. At church that morning, I must admit I was a little skeptical, but that was my nature. I had been to church many times before and really had gotten little or nothing at all out of it. Something happened that morning that had never happened to me before in my life. I felt a spiritual awakening that I thought was left over from last night's alcohol.

My life seemed to change from that point on. I felt at ease with myself and everything around me. That was the moment I figured out what I was missing all those Friday mornings while I had been waiting on my friends' table. All that time there had been a fifth being present. It was Jesus. Who else could it have been?

After that day in church with Brad and his family, everything seemed to be different at home too. I didn't have the need to argue with my girlfriend. Everything seemed to be back to the way it was before all of our fighting had started. It was a real nice relaxed feeling that I had been longing for some time. My prayers had been answered. So were my girlfriend's.

Later on in the week, I got a call from Scott. He had made plans to meet me and Clarke for dinner. The conversation dragged for a while, but then there seemed to be a turn of events. I started feeling more comfortable with them, even though I was still on the skeptical side of the fence. Talking about Jesus and heaven just wasn't what I was used to while eating dinner. Don't get me wrong, the company was great, but I just didn't want to commit my life to anyone or anything at that point. There was something happening, but I still wasn't really sure I wanted to deal with it at the moment. After I left there that night, I couldn't get our conversation out of my head; it was confusing me.

I couldn't sleep that night, but that didn't seem so unusual after all I had been through the past few weeks; sleep didn't come easy. Besides I'm the kind of person who is up and down all night long. It was stormy out, so my cat and I went out to the porch to get some well-deserved air. I was watching the rain come down by the bucketsful and this strange feeling just kept eating away at me. I seemed to be crying inside, actually more like I was dying inside. That's when I decided I couldn't live on my wits alone anymore. It was time to throw out the pride. I asked Jesus to come and take over for me and be my Savior because I just couldn't hang anymore. Lightning was striking, and the rain was coming down, and all the pain that I had in my body was gone. I had just been born again, and I was free of all the chains that were wrapped around my heart and soul. I had never felt such happiness in my entire life. From that night on I had decided to live my life for Christ and to try and be the best I could.

In all my years of waiting tables I got my biggest tip from four Jesus Freaks and the Spirit of Christ.

In all my years of waiting tables I got my biggest tip from four Jesus Freaks and the Spirit of Christ. This is one tip that won't go in my pocket but in my heart, and when I leave the world it will be in my soul.

Three glasses of water and a glass of iced tea gave me a gift that will be with me forever. Brad taught me the ability to learn about Christ and to live for him. Bart showed me how to love Christ and the rest of mankind. Scott gave me the insightful understanding of what is true, right, and enduring. And Clarke bestowed on me the courage to live for Christ no matter what the rest of the world may think. Still the greatest gift of all was from Jesus Christ: Himself, three glasses of water, and a glass of iced tea.

Five to one, and I still came out the winner. I only hope and pray that somewhere out there is a waiter or waitress that will have three glasses of water and a glass of iced tea and be fortunate enough to pick up that tip that will change their life forever as it did mine.

Mike and Angie gave me a new perspective on life. I count them among my friends.

So this story leads us to a few questions: How are we at making friends? How are we at tipping?

How are we at keeping friends? With how many friends from ten years ago are we still in contact? How deep is our understanding of our closest friends? And how deep is their understanding of us?

Are we willing to both encourage and critique our friends for their benefit? Do they feel free to encourage and critique us? And finally, how has the concept of Lewis' Inner Ring intersected our lives?

Let's look more closely at this idea of friendship.

8

FRIENDSHIP AND UNITY

*Affliction's sons are brothers in distress: A brother to relieve --
how exquisite the bliss!*

—Robert Burns.

My friends and I host gatherings around the country, and sometimes around the world. They include student events, men's retreats, prayer gatherings, golf retreats, women's meetings, "vacations with a purpose," or regional gatherings of friends. When I invite friends or acquaintances for the first time, they normally ask what they should expect.

"You should treat it like a treasure hunt," I normally say. "The best part of the weekend might just be the person sitting next to you."

Guests at these gatherings likely will have some sort of significant connection to each other, but they must dig to find it. And when they dig, they find the treasures inside another person: common interests, a favorite place, shared philosophies, mutual friends or family, an idea that will change their lives or, in some cases, a lifetime friendship.

I have been building and collecting friendships intentionally for more than forty years. And I noticed a couple things about these friendships:

- Like a fine wine, they get better with age.
- We get each other's jokes.
- When we are reunited it brings joy.
- We feel understood.
- We talk more deeply and meaningfully than with other, shorter-term relationships.
- We are more likely to sacrifice for each other.

George and I discovered our friendship in 1985. Not only have we continued to be friends over the last three decades, but our wives and children are friends also. I tend to be a bit quirky, as does George.

Yet through the surprises, disappointments, and reconciliations George and I have stuck together. He had the guts to tell me a year ago that he was tired of hearing me talk about writing and that I should get it done. This book is a result of that conversation.

When Pres. Bill Clinton won his first presidential election, much was made of the FOBs (Friends of Bill). Over their lifetime, Bill and his wife Hillary spent their lives building a network of friends throughout the country. During the election, they leaned heavily on their friends to raise money, to build their election team, to stand with them in adversity, and inevitably to celebrate the election win.

Jesus once told a puzzling parable about a dishonest manager who took advantage of his position to make friends so that when he was fired he would find a soft landing. Jesus then tells us the master "commended the dishonest manager for his shrewdness" (Luke 16:8). It seems that maybe using our positions or wealth to make friends might be a good thing.

We have been told our whole lives that money cannot buy friends. We were taught wrong. Money, and other material blessings, can help win friends. Some of my buddies are really good at it. They just seem to watch more closely for the right time, occasion, and gift. And don't we all feel loved when someone is generous to us, or better, invests in us?

We all feel loved when someone invests in us.

I would never suggest that a person try to buy friends with ill motives, but money is one tool that can assist our friend building.

Friends are great at all stages of life, but at the end of life, when we tend to be more reflective and have more needs, that's when we realize how important friends are. They will be the ones at the hospital when we are sick. They'll be the ones bringing us dinners. They will sit with us and understand our hopes and fears. Indeed, they will have become our greatest treasures.

A House United

When I was in college, I read Dr. Robert E. Coleman's book, *The Master Plan of Evangelism*. I became enamored with the idea that if a few people "discipled" a few more people who discipled a few more people, eventually the whole world would be "saved."

Pretty simple, right? Over the course of my life, I realized that this wasn't as simple as Dr. Coleman suggested.

I felt bridled with the heavy burden that my efforts would determine whether or not the world was saved for Jesus. I realize now how ridiculous that sounds, but it was a guilt trip that I carried seriously.

I discovered something twenty-five years ago that changed my view on evangelism. I like it because it comes from one of Jesus' last earthly prayers:

> The glory that you have given me I have given to them [Jesus' disciples], that they may be one even as we are one, I in them and you in me, that they may become perfectly one, so that the world may know that you sent me and love them even as you love me. (John 17:22)

The takeaway from this passage was life-altering for me. It seems that people are drawn into faith more by love and unity than by my guilt trips and the law. (Sounds crazy, right?)

What's fascinating, though, is that Jesus seems to be under the impression that if His people would truly be united, perfectly one, then the whole world would know that God sent Jesus and that God loves them.

Just consider the ramifications. For one, we can drop our guilt trips. The apocalypse won't be determined by them.

A common misconception is that because of all the "rules" in the Scriptures, followers of Jesus best serve him by living constrained, repressed lives. Thinking back, however, I realize that what first drew me in was seeing people who were out-living others. Because it seems that if what Jesus said was true, our lives should stick out, and they should appear desirable.

And they should be entwined with others. We do so much alone. Yet Solomon wrote that two are better than one. I have found this to be profoundly true. If I undertake any given task by myself, it seems to take forever. With a friend working alongside, completion of the task rushes in.

The old adage proves true, "Many hands make quick work."

So unity helps our efficiency in our work life, but other things are required to attain Jesus' idea of becoming "perfectly one" or having perfect unity. John wrote, "If we walk in the light as he is in the light, we have fellowship with one another, and the blood of Jesus his Son cleanses us from all sin" (1 John 1:7).

What does it mean to walk in the light? Mainly we need to involve others in our lives. We need to share deeply, especially our weaknesses, sins, and shortcomings, with others. So when we walk in the light, with God and with others, we are healed, and we become clearly aware that God has forgiven us. This is a critical point: We are forgiven, and we need to believe it.

He forgives us even for the really stupid things that we have done. He forgives us for the things about which we wake up in a cold sweat.

Paul refers to God's people as a body. The body has many parts, and each part has been given a function. Likewise, we have various gifts and talents to be used for the greater good. Practically speaking, this means when we know we're not good at something, we need to bring in a friend.

For instance, I am lousy at matchmaking. I will put two people together who seem a good fit, but they end up not even liking each other. In one case, they argued on their first blind date. So I would like to apologize publicly to all whom I have victimized in their dating lives.

I rarely matchmake anymore, but I have three friends who have the gift. They will set up people whom I believe would never tolerate one another, and somehow the story ends with a happy marriage.

I don't know why they are better at matchmaking than I am. After all, I believe I should be the best matchmaker in the world. After all, I know people deeply and want the best for them. I have discovered, however, that if I find someone ready for marriage, my friends can use their giftedness to help find a better match. And it's much less painful that way – to all concerned.

In this and so many other ways, I have found people who are talented in certain ways for which I have little aptitude. So the closer I can grow to them, and the more friends that I can make, the better connectedness we have as a web of friends.

This web of friends is my version of Paul's body of Christ. So the more friends I have, and the deeper my relationships with each friend, the greater Jesus is in our midst.

Who Puts Unity at Risk?

So what thwarts this unity? It can be our own agendas, our sense of control, our arrogance, our know-it-all nature, our insecurity, our jealousy, or our improper views of the truth.

Paul's prescription for this is humility.

Jesus vacated the highest spot in heaven for the lowest spot on Earth.

Have you ever thought about this? When Jesus left heaven, He vacated the most powerful throne. To become what? A lowly bondservant.

It's difficult to imagine any greater self-emasculation.

And this is exactly why God gave Him the name that is above every name. Have you ever noticed how people react to the name Jesus?

Try an experiment: insert the name of Jesus into casual conversation. You might say, "You know, Jesus said something similar to that." or "Did you ever realize Jesus says that the servants are the greatest of all?" or "What do you think Jesus thinks about that?"

You will find that people will stop in their tracks. This name has taken on power. His name has been exalted above every name (Phil. 2:9). Back in heaven, restored to His kingdom, Jesus once again controls the throne.

No wonder His name tempts us to bow.

> **Sharing our deepest failures and shortcomings draws us closer to our friends, family, and God.**

The buzzword we hear so often today is *vulnerability*. I love it. Twenty years ago, we would have never thought that being vulnerable was a compliment. We would have never agreed that vulnerability is a sign of strength.

We would never think that sharing our deepest failures and shortcomings would draw us closer to our friends, family, and God. Yet now we are discovering the power of vulnerability as we relate to others.

One enemy of vulnerability is judgment. Somehow we believe that when we follow Jesus, it grants us license to judge.

Jesus said just the opposite. According to him, judgment is reserved for God himself. "Judge not, that you be not judged. For with the same judgment you pronounce you will be judged,

and with the measure you use it will be measured to you"
(Matt. 7:1-2).

Who are we to judge our neighbor? Search all the Scriptures
and see if we are encouraged to judge others. Perhaps the closest
is when we told not to "despise prophecies, but test everything"
(1 Thess. 5:20-21).

True, we are to use discretion to place ourselves under good
teaching, but it is hard to resist judging flesh and blood. Discern
teachings, yes. Judge a person, no.

Do you recall the name of the tree in the garden of Eden
of which Adam and Eve were not permitted to eat? It was the
tree of the knowledge of good and evil. It symbolizes one of the
greatest temptations of our time.

We actually believe that we can discern good people from
bad. We believe we can see into a person's heart and judge their
motives. I can't tell you how many times I've been burned when
I attributed motives to a person for something that they never
intended in that way. I became the false accuser.

So how do we promote unity? Don't judge.

Good Leaders Unite

In the Declaration of Independence, Thomas Jefferson set
the stage for national unity: "We hold these truths to be self-
evident, that all men are created equal, that they are endowed by
their Creator with certain unalienable Rights, that among these
are Life, Liberty and the pursuit of Happiness."

What seems obvious to us today shook the world. How
can all men be created equal? Are there really unalienable rights
that everyone deserves? Should we really be given liberty? Is the
pursuit of happiness important or just absurd hedonism?

So Jefferson and his cronies didn't just say such crazy things, they added, "we mutually pledge to each other our Lives, our Fortunes and our sacred Honor." Translation: They risked everything. We could learn from them.

Here's a definition of leadership from guru John Maxwell that can infuse unity into any given group: "Leadership is when someone finds noble principles and follows them with such conviction and sacrifice that others can't help but follow."

The Scriptures tell us that all authority on heaven and Earth has been established by God. I find it hard to believe about the worst—Pharaoh, Hitler, Stalin—but few question that Lincoln was sent by God Himself.

Abraham Lincoln talked about unity in the middle of a war that raged between the North and South. Cousins were matched against cousins, sometimes brothers against brothers. The nation was ripped apart in a way that none of us can fathom. And there stood Abraham Lincoln in the middle, a tall but slender man, with an inspired understanding of unity.

Here's what he said: "Both [sides] read the same Bible, and pray to the same God; and each invokes his aid against the other," he said in his second inaugural address. "Prayers of both could not be answered."

Lincoln bared the most absurd hypocrisy of the time. How could anyone ask for God's aid to defeat his kin in the bloodiest war in American history? If we read the same Bible and pray to the same God, shouldn't it be easy for us to unite? If we share similar values, why not stand together and put aside any differences that may divide us?

True leadership is humble, noble, requires conviction and sacrifice, and must be immersed in kindness. Leadership yearns for unity. And people yearn for someone to follow. This scenario is never clearer than in American elections. During any given presidential election season, we believe that one of the candidates can truly save the country. They all fail to varying degrees, but we put our hope in them regardless.

When I played high school football, a collision with an oversized tackle left me with a pinched nerve in my neck. Whenever I hit someone, my right arm went numb. My injury required that I sit out the season. So I watched my buddies win the state championship game from the sidelines, in a neck brace.

My body had been taken out of the game because of a small piece of cartilage displaced against a nerve in my neck. Even so, one small piece of disunity hurts the entire cause. As the great poet and preacher John Donne wrote: "No man is an island / Entire of itself / Every man is a piece of the continent / A part of the main."

Jesus must have encountered serious disunity. When He walked into a town, people automatically divided themselves between supporters and detractors. In fact, William Barclay, in his *New Testament Commentary*, said this: "The plain fact is that if Simon the Zealot [one of Jesus' disciples] had met Matthew the tax gatherer [another disciple] anywhere else than in the company of Jesus, he would have stuck a dagger in him."

When Jesus chose His disciples, He knew that Simon and Matthew would hate each other. He chose them anyway. Then He helped them work through their differences. In the end, they became part of a united core of young men, though not until after Jesus' departure.

Speaking Truth Boldly but Kindly

We should concern ourselves with how we communicate.

The Scriptures exhort us to "speak the truth in love" (Eph. 4:15). What does this really mean? And if we learned this form of communication, would we come off as too soft? Aren't these two thoughts mutually exclusive? How can a person be boldly honest and kind at the same time?

We see examples of errors on either end of the spectrum: someone too weak to tell the truth or someone brutally harsh in their directness, or saying something simply untruthful.

A counselor friend of mine used to distinguish between Blue Zone communication and Red Zone communication. In the Blue Zone, people are calm, emotions are in check, communication is well-thought-out, and the conversation generally ends well.

In the Red Zone, however, emotions peak, tempers are unleashed, the language becomes sharp and biting. Those conversations end badly.

So how should a person approach conflict? Fortunately, I've had the opportunity to witness Blue Zone communication firsthand.

My friend Marty is perhaps the most critical person I know, but he's also kind (most of the time). Those who know him come to appreciate his observations—even if not at first. They've come to trust that what he says is true and probably needs to be heard.

I once watched Marty confront a national leader about neglecting his son. Following this episode, the leader actually thanked Marty for challenging him. I believe this level of direct communication challenges most of us. I often leave a conversation wishing I had either not said something so boldly or wishing I said anything instead of nothing.

The apostle James instructs us to "Be quick to hear, slow to speak, slow to anger" (James 1:19). I find most people to be just the opposite: slow to listen,

> **"Be quick to hear, slow to speak, and slow to anger"** —James 1:19.

quick to speak, and quick to anger. We all speak too quickly. We use tones that we really don't intend.

Conflict or disunity arises quickly in these cases. Feathers are ruffled when we are hasty or careless in our approach. It seems that in order to deliver truth, we must establish a relational precedent rooted in love. The other person must feel cared for by us in order to receive straight talk.

It requires patience and discipline to communicate the way James suggests.

Building and Maintaining Strong Relationships

Threats await our beloved friendships. Conflict, tension, and bitterness work their way in. Offenses may be taken, even when they were not intended. Miscommunication, insecurity, and jealousy can threaten our relationships. When friendships go sour, in most cases, we are too quick to write them off, to conclude that they are no longer necessary or are simply too painful to continue.

So in our Western, disposable culture, we throw these treasures away.

Jesus intends us to view relationships differently. He says, "If you are offering your gift at the altar and there remember that your brother has something against you, leave your gift there before the altar and go. First be reconciled to your brother, and then come and offer your gift" (Matt. 5:23-24).

To the ancient Jew, few things were more important than presenting sacrifices at the altar. Through these sacrifices, sins were forgiven and relationship with God was restored. Yet Jesus tells His followers that they should cease from this important custom if they found themselves unreconciled with anyone. Throughout Jesus' teachings, He values relationships deeply. He desires that we do the same.

Let's consider two examples. The first man treats his relationships as disposable. Over the course of his life he leaves behind his best friends, maybe even family members. As he grows older, fewer and fewer of his friends have history with him. They don't understand him or rightly value him. Through the years, he becomes a lonely, bitter old man. He seems grumpy.

The second man decides at a young age that he will attempt to preserve all of his relationships, especially his closest ones, and including the difficult ones. This single decision inflicts great pain over his life.

Still he remains faithful, even to those who hurt him. He reconciles with them regularly.

As the years pass, he finds ways to include his old friends in his newer interests. Together, the friends might attend certain events together or intentionally plan ways to connect their wives and children.

This person stays connected, whether it be with his neighbors, his career relationships, or his church. He makes new friends while cherishing old ones. As life goes on, he becomes the eternal optimist. People love to be around him. He lives a meaningful, enjoyable, and long life.

Research tells us the people who live into their nineties share one vital characteristic: their undaunted optimism. You see, we were created with the need to be connected to other humans. We "die on the vine" when we have no community.

Jesus knew this when He coached us to handle our friendships. If we continue to reconcile—ask forgiveness and forgive—it frees our soul from the bitterness that would otherwise harden us.

Bitterness affects more than just our mood. Studies show that those who are chronically angry and bitter are more susceptible to cancer. One could say that holding a grudge against another person is like drinking poison and hoping the other person dies.

When I was in college, I was quite the Bible thumper. Some in my fraternity house appreciated it, others didn't. At the top of the list of my adversaries was Chris. It was not hard for me to tell that Chris loathed me. He avoided eye contact. He never sat at my table during meals. Any conversation was cut short.

He clearly did not like me.

One night I read Jesus' admonition to make peace with my brothers. Chris, my fraternity *brother*, immediately came to mind. I had made a decision at the time to not let the sun go down on my anger, as the Scriptures urge.

Since there was no way out, I somehow had to make peace with Chris. I rolled around in bed for about three hours trying to ignore my own convictions, and the urging of the Spirit. In the end, I rose angrily and told the Lord, "Okay, I'll call him. But when I wake him up and he's angry, it's all Your fault!"

Since I lived in an apartment, I decided to call the fraternity house phone. I had Chris' direct phone number, but I didn't have the guts to call it. If I called the house phone and he was in bed (which he certainly would have been at 1 a.m. on a school night), I felt that I would be off the hook.

When I called the house, the phone rang three or four times. One of the guys answered. I asked if I could talk to Chris, and the person began to tell me that he was surely in bed. But then he suddenly stopped. "Wait—. Chris actually just came out of the restroom. He's right here." I couldn't believe it. So much for my strategy.

"Chris," I said, "I have been tossing and turning for three hours because I am not at peace with you. I realize that I'm a hypocrite, I don't always live out what I say, and I know you don't respect me because of that. I would like to ask your forgiveness for all the times I acted holier-than-thou. I'm sorry for the way I treated you."

Something seemed to break loose on the other end of the line.

"Are you telling me that you've been lying in bed for three hours thinking about me?" Chris asked. "You're right. I always thought you were a hypocrite. But this phone call means a lot to me."

Although Chris and I did not become best friends, we made significant strides, and I think we actually began to appreciate one another. We somehow turned the tide of toxicity into a newfound unity.

Years later, my wife, Beth, and I raised four children. We love our children. They have all grown up and have chosen extraordinary husbands and wives. As they were growing up, I unfortunately cast a long shadow over their lives. I was editor of the local paper, then the general manager of another.

I was active in church, taught Sunday school, and was an elder. I was involved with students alongside various governors doing forums on faith and values.

From time to time, I noticed a somber mood over a couple of my sons. I thought perhaps they felt it might be difficult to measure up to lofty expectations. A crazy idea came to mind: "What if I told them in detail about my worst failure?" Just thinking about the incident of betrayal brought pangs of guilt. I decided to tell them anyway.

So, over the next six weeks, I picked a time and place for each child (then teenagers), to tell them my greatest blunder. Each meeting was emotional. One child had a hundred questions. Another tried to console me for it. Another simply wept, and another one decided it was a suitable time to confess all his shortcomings to me.

We happened to be meeting in the hot tub, so as the confessions came one after another, I found myself dehydrated. I paused for a long drink of water, and then continued listening to the list.

With each child, the experience took on a different mood. But in every case, it brought our relationship to a new level. When they realized that their father was capable of the worst, somehow they were comforted about their own lives.

In each case, those relationships took a turn for the better. Today, I'm grateful that I have a connection with my children. I realize that this is not always the case. Divisions in families seem epidemic. It requires hard work to maintain unity, and we often fail.

I try to never take it for granted that our family members love each other. But whenever I think of the bond that I share with my children, I think back to my confession.

So whatever the difficult relationship, remember the power of confession and reconciliation. It will bind you to that person.

The Art of Communication

Where do the foibles of communication become more public than in modern media? Issues are taken out of context. Blame is administered without any proof or evidence. Opinion is swallowed by the population without the necessary fact-checking, causing reputations irreparable damage.

After spending eighteen years in newspaper and radio organizations, I had a front-row seat to some of the best and worst communication imaginable. I came to one conclusion: for all we think we know about communication, we are bad at it. Especially with the proliferation of social media, our bad habits multiply.

We hamstring our communication by removing one sense after another from our messages. It is no wonder that counties, cities, states, and countries move from unity to separation to alienation.

Lest we forget, listening and paying attention remain the bedrock of good communication. Somehow, we must check our own politics, philosophies, and other personal background at the door, so we can hear someone as he or she intended. We seldom repeat back what we have heard to make sure we understand the message (which is perhaps the best way to actively listen, and to gather information).

We should remind ourselves of James' advice: "be quick to hear, slow to speak, and slow to anger" (James 1:19). James gets it. Wouldn't we all be better off if we listened more than we spoke? The old adage is, "God gave us two ears and one mouth for a reason."

We must improve our listening. It pays to take time to get to know someone, to sit down with them face-to-face and to have an in-depth and thorough conversation. Most of our communication today prohibits all of these. I believe Gregory Spencer got it right when he said:

> Silly as it sounds, we might improve authenticity by counting the number of human senses available in our communication—and "lean toward" the choice with the higher number. Face-to-face has the potential to include all five. A video phone call loses touch. A regular phone call loses sight. Voicemail loses hearing. E-mail loses tone of voice. For all its benefits, e-mail has been the cause of untold confusion and conflict. Real presence understands that we are sensory creatures. The likelihood of misunderstanding grows exponentially with each lost sense.[5]

As I think about this topic, one memory stands out.

It is a simple picture. I saw three teenage girls walking at the mall. All three were talking exuberantly into their cell phones. I had to wonder what great lengths their mothers or fathers went to in order to place all three girls at the same location so they could be together. Yet they could have just as easily ignored each other and had the same conversations with the same other people at home.

Somehow we have traded good communication for a cheap substitute. Great communication touches all the senses. We used to say that 93 percent of communication is nonverbal. I don't hear that much anymore because so little communication today is verbal.

I marvel at scenes today where dozens of people are milling about in the same room, but each one is staring like a zombie at his or her smartphone. Can we really be much of an enlightened generation when this becomes the main avenue for exchanging thoughts and ideas?

An old friend of mine who works extensively with young men dares them to become a Renaissance Man. He tells them to stop using e-mail and text messages. Instead, he exhorts them to write personal, handwritten notes. Just the thought of receiving a personal, handwritten note feels good to the soul. These notes are often read multiple times. A good thank-you note or a good love letter brings an added degree of connection.

Although it is not always possible, face-to-face communication flows with the stimulation of every sense. We understand others more deeply when we study them, their reactions, their facial expressions, their voice inflection, the nodding of the head, the brightening of the eyes, and the gesturing of hands. Thinking about this makes me long for the days of Renaissance men.

Once we receive a message, how should we respond? Few of us realize how much our language has digressed during our lifetime. Just for fun, Google Abraham Lincoln's Gettysburg Address:

> Four score and seven years ago our fathers brought forth
> on this continent, a new nation, conceived in liberty, and
> dedicated to the proposition that all men are created equal.

Do you know anyone who talks that way? And which would you prefer, Lincoln's prose or the monosyllabic blabber used by most of us?

I teach writing. Some consider it a dead art, although it seems that most employers I know are looking for a good writer or two. A young man or woman can move quickly up the corporate totem pole simply by proper English usage.

Opportunities abound to increase our communication skills. There are classes, lexicons, handbooks, opportunities on the Internet, books to read. The more we expose ourselves to great literature and great speeches, the better we will communicate.

So give it a try. Become a Renaissance Man.

9

RECONCILIATION

In essentials unity, in nonessentials liberty, in all things charity.

—Augustine

hy do we choose to fight over tiny, inconsequential issues when an apology can disarm the situation?

Jesus hammers home a higher priority: to resolve any present conflicts. Indeed, getting right with our fellow man is urgent to God.

If we really want to learn the art of friendship, we must learn how to heal rifts. So why do we refuse to apologize? Is it pride? Embarrassment? Or just plain stubbornness? Perhaps we've never been taught how.

Whatever the case, in the end, it's up to us to pick ourselves up by the scruff of the neck, go to those whom we've offended, and find a way to make a sincere apology. Any sincere apology should go something like, "I am sorry. I was wrong. Would you forgive me?" Such an apology touches all the bases: an admission of regret, an admission of fault, and a request to be forgiven.

It is okay to tell the person how we feel about any given offense. We should master the art of the "When you ___ I feel ___" sentence. Somehow we feel validated that the other person knows how we feel. On the other side, it's important

> **A sincere apology should admit regret, admit fault, and request to be forgiven.**

for us to know how the wounded person feels.

Eventually, we all need to reach the place where we say we are sorry. My friends and I have a 90/10 rule. That means if I am only 10 percent wrong, I should apologize. Obviously, when we feel like we're 90 percent wrong, mustering an apology might be easier—or might not. In order to restore a relationship completely, both sides need to understand the other, and both sides need to own up to their responsibility.

"It takes two to Tango," my mother said frequently to her children. At least two parties must participate in order to have conflict.

While working at the newspaper plant, I tried to take a daily walkabout. That meant visiting each department and checking in with the manager and a few employees. When there was tension, it could be cut with a knife. Usually, it made itself known in two stone faces that refused to look at each other. If I felt the tension just walking in, imagine how the other employees felt.

Or worse, customers.

So we would make our way through the "making up" session. Each side would tell how they felt, and each side would

be given the opportunity to apologize. Then each was given the
opportunity to forgive. That was always the hardest part.

The Art of Forgiveness

Forgiveness emerges more easily when responding to a true
and sincere apology.

Once we apologize, we should stop talking. It's amazing
how many times someone wants to get in one last "ugh" or eye
roll or any other preschool-type reaction. Any such expression
negates any degree of sincerity that came with the apology.

I said it earlier. I'll say it again. We seldom realize how easy
it is to apologize, rather than to start a fight, or to continue a
feud, or more sadly, to end a relationship.

But why is it so hard to forgive? Sometimes the apology is
insincere. Sometimes the person refuses to validate our feelings.
Some days we've slept on the offense so many times that it has
been blowing up in our minds, occupying more space than it
should.

I found a few things that help when I feel someone has
committed a seemingly unforgivable sin against me:

- First, it helps to say it: "I forgive you."
- Second, we should take some time to remember all
  that has been forgiven us. We don't have to dwell
  too long on our own imperfections to realize that
  perhaps the offense wasn't as bad as we thought. In
  fact, we are perfectly capable of offending others in
  this same way.
- Third, if those don't work, pray for 100 percent
  forgiveness. With each stage of forgiveness, we

normally forgive a certain percentage of the total offense. I'm actually doing pretty well if I hit 30, 40 or even 50 percent forgiveness. But that still leaves a lot of sludge in the pipe. We operate best when the pipe is clean, 100 percent clean.

- Fourth, we must learn to forget. The more we stew over any given offense, the more it bothers us. Lack of forgiveness haunts the person who refuses to forgive. I have found that most times, the originator of the offense has no idea what stress and anxiety the offense has put on its victim who refuses to forgive.
- Fifth, and this may be the most important one, we need to believe we have forgiven the offender and act like it in the days, weeks, and months ahead.

We need to understand that forgiveness cleanses us from deep-seeded bitterness. Otherwise, every parent on Earth would not push their children to reconcile.

Like anything else, however, we need constant remedial work. Through this work we can live a peaceful and rich life. When I think about the phrase "grumpy old man," I think of bitter old souls who are tense, judgmental, and harsh.

On the other side are old men who live free, easy, and peaceful lives. The greatest difference between these two fates is forgiveness. The one who forgives is healthier and happier than the one who refuses.

Harboring unresolved anger creates chronic anxiety, which keeps the body in a

Harboring unresolved anger creates chronic anxiety.

state of high alert. Hormones produce excess adrenaline and cortisol with stress, depleting our body's cytotoxic T cells, natural killer "foot soldiers" in the fight against cancer, as cited by cancer researcher Dr. Michael Barry, author of the book "The Forgiveness Project."

Forgiveness therapy is now being pioneered as a new form of treatment used to reduce the chance of cancer in high-risk patients, as reported by Dr. Steven Standiford, chief of surgery at the Cancer Treatment Centers of America. He maintains that unforgiveness "makes people sick and keeps them that way."[6]

An Unrepentant Offender

So what must I do, you may ask, if my offender refuses to apologize? First, our forgiveness should not depend on whether or not we have received a real apology. Sure, an apology makes it easier. Friendships are more easily restored with an apology.

This is definitely true for marriages. But unavoidably, there are times when the other person simply won't apologize. Holding a grudge against this person is no less toxic than refusing to forgive an apology.

What if the person who offended me is dead? you may ask. This is perhaps the most difficult question. More so, what if the offender was one of my parents? Or worse, both my parents?

At age thirty-three, I reconciled with my father about something he did that offended me. I had held it against him for years. Finally, I apologized for holding the grudge for so long. We had a long conversation in which he asked how I felt, how it made me act toward him, and how deeply it hurt.

That took some guts on his part. But in the end, he said this: "You know, Brad, there comes a time in every man's life when he must forgive his father. There are no perfect fathers or mothers."

I still find his thought profound. Every father and every mother has wounded their children emotionally, either consciously or unconsciously, or both. So forgiveness is required.

How does God allow such a painful state to exist? Perhaps He hopes we will eventually find the Father who loves His children perfectly. Naturally, such a quest involves pain, but in the end, we receive the loving embrace of the heavenly Father.

I believe Dad to be correct. We must all forgive and attempt to reconcile with our parents. For our own good. No father or mother is perfect. And hopefully their imperfections turn our focus to the perfect One. This proves especially true for fathers and sons. Father wounds are epidemic.

Jay

When Jay was ten years old, his father left his mother and family. So Jay grew up with his mom, and later stepfather, who loved him and gave him all the advantages of life.

As Jay told a small group of us his story, I was captured by one specific element: he described in great detail the red go-kart he found parked in the front yard on his twelfth birthday. His face grew red as he explained that his father had left the go-kart in the front yard and didn't have the decency to knock on the door or try to see him.

I had a different reaction. Somehow, in the midst of this awful story, the go-kart became the great ray of hope. "That's the only way the man knew how to show the son that he loved him," I thought.

Later that night, after Jay's story, I found myself in a conversation with him. He had been tremendously open with us, and we all appreciated his honesty. Yet I couldn't get the red go-kart out of my brain. I found myself saying to Jay, "I look forward to meeting your dad."

"You mean my stepdad," he rattled back.

"No, I actually mean your biological dad," I said.

Jay grew flustered, and anger burned on his face. He did not know what to say. Over the course of the next year the other mentors and I had any number of conversations with Jay about his family. The topic of his father was seldom a positive conversation.

One positive conversation for Jay took place when he met another mentor, Steve Largent, the Hall of Fame football player for the Seattle Seahawks. Steve's father had also abandoned his family during Steve's early years growing up in Oklahoma.

Here's what Jay said recently about their conversation:

"During the internship, I spoke with Steve Largent about forgiving my father. He made a clear distinction between forgiveness and reconciliation. He told me that God calls us to forgive, and that brings healing in our lives.

"That is our responsibility. It takes two people to have true reconciliation, which does not always happen. He told me that the most important thing was the condition of my heart toward my father on Earth as well as my Father in heaven.

"Somehow our relationships on Earth are closely connected to our relationships spiritually."

Once Steve had this conversation with Jay, he began asking us more about how to reconcile broken relationships. We talked at length about what it would take to repair a relationship. At first we were simply speaking hypothetically, then later we began to talk more and more specifically about his dad.

After a couple months of this, Jay came to me and said he was ready to meet his father. It blew my mind. I was so proud of him. This was somehow going to work out. I couldn't help but remember the red go-kart.

We decided that Jay would invite his father and stepmom to come visit us in Annapolis. As the day grew closer, I found myself more and more nervous about the meeting. I can't imagine what Jay felt like. He asked me if I would join him to meet his dad. So we picked a private, neutral place and asked the father and his wife to meet us on a Saturday morning.

Words cannot exaggerate the awkwardness of that meeting. The father, a strong and imposing figure, entered the room with his wife. All the oxygen drained out.

Jay, to his credit, stood up and approached his dad and shook his hand.

The hulking father immediately transformed into a sobbing mess. He couldn't even talk. We invited him to sit down at the table. His wife sat next to him.

Jay began to explain to his dad that he wanted to rekindle, or perhaps *kindle* would be the right word, a new relationship. Jay had hardly started speaking when his father again broke into sobs. It took what seemed an eternity for the father to gather himself enough to respond.

"I've dreamed about this day ever since I left the family," the father explained. "I think about you every day. I love you so much, and I never knew how I could communicate that to you."

We then witnessed an outpouring of love from Jay, his dad, and Jay's stepmom.

In the months that followed, Jay and his father became intentional about talking to each other regularly. They spoke on the phone every day. Now, years later, they have forged a strong and powerful bond with each other.

Jay is a better man for having embraced the painful part of his history. From that place, the Lord performed perhaps one of the most amazing pieces of redemption I have ever witnessed.

Like Jay and his father, all men are invited to reconcile across this divide. And we must surrender to this process no matter how deep or how long the offense has existed. One cannot imagine the blessing a son will encounter when he reconciles with his father.

Dominic

Like Jay, Dominic came to Annapolis as a part of our nine-month internship program. He arrived in the fall of 2009. Dominic told his story in one of his early sessions with the mentors.

Bravely, he went into great detail. Dominic had been raised by his grandparents for a number of reasons. First, his mother, who had a brain injury from a car accident, needed help from her parents physically to conduct her life. Second, his father later had left during his teen years.

It was at that point of the story that Dominic began to cry. He told us about the conversation he had with his dad before he left the family. Dominic was a high school student. His father, a night shift worker at the prison, woke him at 5:30 a.m. to tell him he was leaving for good.

As it turns out, Dominic's dad believed that he was meant to be a woman. He told Dominic that he was going to have a sex change operation, leave Colorado and the family, and they would never see him again.

He left.

Dominic showed his courage in other ways during the internship, and we came to know, love, and respect him. He made good friends, he asked good questions, and he was all-in for the activities.

One of those friends was Blazer.

Fast-forward to a few years after the internship. In December 2011, Dominic and Blazer decided to do everything in their power to reunite Dominic with his dad. Blazer searched the Internet and found him in North Carolina. Dominic wrote a letter asking to meet him. He agreed to meet.

Knowing that a meeting might be awkward, Blazer went on his own to check out Dominic's dad. He found out several interesting pieces of information: First, Dominic's dad had tried to commit suicide in 2003. Second, he met Jesus in a life-altering way. Third, he had joined a home church of Cameroon refugees because other churches turned him away. Finally, he had befriended the pastor, who helped him become a pastor himself.

Because Blazer lived nearby, he visited a few times.

In 2014, Dominic went on a work trip. When he realized he'd be a couple hours from his dad, he set up a surprise visit with Blazer. One can only imagine the emotion when Dominic entered the house to see his father for the first time in eleven years!

Dominic and his dad reconnected and have stayed in contact.

Like Jay, Dominic embraced his dad, and the two rekindled their relationship. Dominic is now married and is a father himself. He stays connected with his fellow intern friends and has experienced healing from his earlier pain.

Rarely does one pass through life unscathed of "father wounds." If Jay and Dominic could face and work through the wounds from their fathers, it is hard to imagine that any of us has a decent excuse not to.

Dominic's story has caused me to push all of our young men back toward their fathers—no matter what. Time and time again I have watched a father and son move from hurt and separation to supernatural restoration.

Learning how to apologize and learning how to forgive become the blocking and tackling of friendships. With practice, we can get better at either or both.

Some people are gifted. They can get to the apology quickly and sincerely. Likewise, some have the gift of forgiving. They are quick to forget the offense and move on. Either way, those who take the high road will live a more fulfilling life.

It pays to start early.

One important note: In cases of abuse, I do not recommend that a son or daughter expose themselves to more damage until a relationship with Dad can be safe. No one expects children to expose themselves to more abuse while seeking to restore a fatherly relationship. In these cases, prayer for healing is essential until a safe environment is created.

While a father-son relationship is unique, the principles are the same with friendships. We should strive for unity in all our relationships and whenever possible make reconciliation a goal.

AUTHORITY

The Scriptures make four things clear regarding authority:
1. It belongs to God.
2. It has been given to Jesus.
3. Jesus lends it out according to His purposes.
4. We are to submit to authority.

A friend of mine, Tim, is a student of worldly authority. He tells the story about coaching his son's junior high school basketball team. When his team started practice, he would instruct the players how to perform their various roles.

He went to great lengths to be specific about movement, passing, shooting, and such. Yet when the next practice came around, each player had regressed to his original ways. None of the new techniques were sticking.

Tim noticed some parents came to the practice and were sitting in the stands observing his every move. Perhaps some strategic parental manipulation was working behind the scenes.

He had an idea.

After practice, Tim huddled the team and gave them one directive: "Every time your parents drive you to or from a practice, you must say, 'thank you.' "

Over the next several practices, Tim noticed a change in the bleachers. The parents smiled more often. They seemed to give Tim more compliments. When the players saw that their parents respected the coach, they did too. Their attention to Tim's coaching improved, along with their play.

Remember, all authority on heaven and earth has been given to Jesus, and we see the use of that authority in different ways throughout Scripture. Tim understood that his players belonged under the authority of their parents. So he chose to tap into that authority in order to lead the young basketball team.

In creation, clearly God is the authority. Throughout the Old Testament, authority and the Holy Spirit were given to certain leaders for certain purposes. Often, the authority, and also the Spirit, were taken away when the purpose was complete.

In the New Testament, Paul exhorts his friends to pray for those in authority so that his cohorts may "lead a peaceful and quiet life" (1 Tim. 2:2). Paul also instructs them to submit to authorities. This can prove difficult, especially in a democracy. But that doesn't change the fact that we are to pray for, and submit to, those in authority.

If any of us had a friend who had been granted a powerful position, we would hang out with him or her every moment we could. Yet we neglect Jesus, despite the fact that He possesses all authority. Go figure.

So then it becomes our mission to figure out how authority plays itself out in our earthly classroom. Whenever we enter a room, someone occupies the place of authority. Whether we like it or not, his or her authority is derived from Jesus. In recognition of the source of all authority, it would only make sense for us to introduce ourselves to that person and befriend him or her.

When it comes time to bow to authority, we often chafe. We don't like to submit, and we're not very good at it. Learning to submit depends on first understanding those two things about ourselves.

If God is God, who controls the authorities on earth, He requires that we learn how to submit. Throughout the centuries, there are those who have rebelled to cast off rulers unworthy of their authority. These can be good causes or not.

Perhaps the most honorable rebellion came from Dr. Martin Luther King Jr. and the African-Americans who brought Mahatma Gandhi's art of peaceful protest to America. They protested peacefully for their rights, often exposing themselves to brutal punishment by the authorities.

In the end, they moved their cause forward, gaining new rights and equalities. The fruits of their labors are still being worked out today, as "We hold these truths to be self-evident, that all men are created equal, that they are endowed by their Creator with certain unalienable Rights, that among these are Life, Liberty and the pursuit of Happiness." (Declaration of Independence)

10

VIRTUE AND CHARACTER

I hold the precepts of Jesus as delivered by Himself, to be the most pure, benevolent, and sublime which have ever been preached to man. I adhere to the principles of the first age.

—Thomas Jefferson

What defines you? When a person says your name, what images are conjured up? Are you helpful? Attractive? Lazy? Encouraging? Bitter? Athletic? Intelligent? Knowledgeable? Feisty? Rebellious? Bubbly?

Next question: Is the collection of adjectives that just came to mind the sum total of your identity? Is it the image God created for you? Have you ever considered who you really are? Even at my age, I've found that certain friends still haven't grounded themselves in their true identity. It is these people who lose their footing when midlife, and its crises, come crashing in.

Are we living out God's version of us or some concoction of our own, born of a patchwork of our favorite personalities stitched together? I must admit, I often compare my life to others, then try to incorporate their best into my own identity.

Paul sees it differently: "For you have died, and your life is hidden with Christ in God. When Christ who is your life appears, then you also will appear with him in glory" (Col. 3:3-4).

A teacher of mine used to say, "You can be born twice and die once, or you can be born once and die twice." The truth is, when we invite the Holy Spirit into our hearts, we die. Even as Jesus died and was resurrected, so do we start a new life as a temple of the Holy Spirit. When this occurs, our life goes directly to the throne of God. It is then we begin to be transformed by the renewing of our minds. The heart changes instantly, the brain takes more time—a lifetime, really.

Yet, if we want to embrace our intended personality, we need to set our minds on things above. In this place we find our authentic selves.

> **Our life on Earth is not the most important part of our life.**

Distracting as it may be, our life on Earth is not the most important part of our life. It is in the kingdom of God where we fully become who we were intended to be, not unlike Adam and Eve when they were first created. I believe we will be astounded by our new heavenly bodies.

So as we look up, and fix our eyes on Jesus, we find the person who we were intended to be. One way we measure this process is to review what turns us on, what makes us feel important, popular, handsome, strong or trustworthy. When we take an inventory of ourselves, it's not long before we find what drives us, and therefore our identity.

Establish Your Identity in Love

As we mature, hopefully we find ways to file off the jagged edges—the sins, bad habits, bad judgment, spite. These are the things that God never designed for us, but the fall of man has brought, to some degree, into every personality. Hopefully, the Lord is exposing these pieces to us, and we are awake enough to notice them.

Some are sleep walking. They don't self-evaluate. They don't stop and take stock of themselves, weighing which of their parts were either intended or not intended by God.

I have found that the older I get, the more I become aware of the non-purposeful things that are attached to me, the things that have become habit and are difficult to overcome. Yet I have also found that my awareness of these things has grown, until at one time I return to my fallen Humpty Dumpty state.

God Himself exudes love. God is love. If allowed, He will permeate every part of you with His love; indeed, a new identity sets in.

When I was in high school I knew a girl named Anne. We went to the same church. She was a popular girl yet was known for caring about others. I witnessed this firsthand on a ski trip with our youth group.

Anne was by far the best skier in the group and a senior. Yet whenever I saw her on the ski slope she was picking someone up or giving them instructions or encouraging them before whisking down to the bottom of the mountain where she would get on the lift up and start over again.

A senior took care of sophomores. I thought, "Nobody cares about sophomores!" Somehow she seemed to enjoy it. I marveled at this wonderful example of God's love working through someone.

I believe that if I had as much talent, I would be so busy showing off that I would view those struggling on the slopes around me simply as obstacles. I was struck by the difference in the way she treated others. By viewing this spectacle, and a number of other examples of love over the weekend, I saw Jesus and His thoughts in a new way.

He was simply too magnetic, too loving, too good, too caring, too much interested in the things deep in our souls.

The gospel writer Luke portrays Mary and Martha as two more examples of identity. Martha, the busy one, bustled about the house taking care of company. She took care of the visible things: the dinner, the hosting, the chores associated with hospitality.

Mary, on the other hand, seemed to put everything aside, and focused on Jesus and His teachings. Which woman had the right idea? We don't have to look far to find out. Jesus Himself told Martha that Mary had chosen the "good portion" or better way (Luke 10:42).

What we devote our time and attention to makes us uniquely us. Mary and Martha had a choice. They could focus on Jesus, or they could focus on any number of other distractions. How is your focus? Is it singly on Jesus, or on the myriad of problems that surround you?

Over time, I have learned that love is a person. And that person is Jesus. He is still very much alive, and He is alive in my life. He talks, I listen. Then I talk and He listens. Sometimes neither one of us talk.

Mother Teresa was once asked, "What do you say to God when you pray?"

"I don't say anything. I just listen," she responded.

"So what does God say?" the person asked.

"He doesn't say anything. He just listens."

With all my brain I cannot understand what she meant by this. But somehow what she said strikes me as true. Somehow when we fellowship with God, words simply don't suffice.

Paul writes that when we pray, the Holy Spirit "intercedes for us with groanings too deep for words" (Rom. 8:26). We do our best with our words, but sometimes communication must go deeper. It must come from the depths of our souls, and it requires the aid of the Holy Spirit to properly translate for God. It's not possible for us to fully comprehend what God is communicating with us. Someday we'll be able to comprehend everything that He intends for us, but that day is not today. Now we must settle for glimpses, reflections, pieces of the grand whole. Sometimes the Holy Spirit must translate. Each and every day we're putting them together, and the connections are life-giving.

Everything Jesus said and did is love. So was Jesus showing love when He grabbed a whip and drove the money changers out of the temple? Hard to say, yet it must be so. He is capable of only love. So whether we see him handling the money changers, or raising someone from the dead, both are motivated by great love.

When we love others the way Jesus did, the whole world sees Jesus. Jesus laid down His life for others, and we ought to lay down our lives moment by moment. We can show no greater love than to care for another before ourselves.

> **When we love others the way Jesus did, the whole world sees Jesus.**

So we are given the opportunity to both embrace God's love, and to pass it on to those around us. The picture that enters my mind is one of living water running over a three-tiered fountain. When I am fully able to receive it, His living water gushes onto the top level, then onto those around it. It never ceases, no matter how long and intensely it flows. Notably, I am rarely in that state. Yet that's what I desire. And I believe that's how Jesus operated.

God is love, and He requires that we return that love to Him. When we do this, those around us can't help but take notice. Jesus takes it from there. So when we think about our identity, what if we made the decision, as Mary did, to focus all our love and attention on Jesus?

What if those around us noticed? What if love became our defining quality? What if our "inner ring" was defined by love? Who could resist?

No one that I have yet met.

Leave Things Better Than You Found Them

The interns we oversee in Washington, DC, sometimes take road trips. We set these trips up. We plan them so the group can meet our best friends and see the things going on around the country and around the world.

We always send them off with a bit of trepidation. What if they behave badly while they're with our friends? What if they leave the house a mess? What if they don't help out? What if they offend the friend?

Each time we send them, we trust the interns to behave wisely. Usually we give them a grand lecture about how to be good guests. The art of being a good guest begins with the thought: "Leave things better than you found them."

Truthfully, we would be happy if they just didn't leave things worse than they found them. Yet a higher standard seems appropriate.

It doesn't take long for us to get feedback. Sometimes it's for something as simple as emptying the dishwasher or helping prepare a meal or fixing something that is broken or spending some quality time with the host's children.

When the interns engage well with their hosts, our friends tell us about it.

We have found that this formula makes for long and meaningful relationships: Interns visit. They engage their hosts. They help out. They end up with lasting friendships. It's one of our favorite things to connect two friends and see what happens.

Oftentimes, God does His best work and creates a win-win situation in these meetings. But nowhere do we see it more than when we send our interns home for Christmas. Without fail, parents notice. So they tell us, "John actually made his bed."

"Chris took out the trash without being asked."

"Colin helped with the dishes."

"Andrew actually began a conversation about values."

The parents are spellbound. They simply can't believe that in five short months, their sons gained such amazing skills, when they'd spent years trying to train them. (There's no secret formula here. Young men often respond better to mentors than parents.)

So we actually make it a motto for life: "Leave things better than you found them."

Pick up some trash, wipe down the toilet, cook a meal, fill up a car with gas, bring a sick person a meal, buy a gift for the host when you leave, the list goes on and on.

Even writing a thank-you note has become old-fashioned. We encourage young men to write handwritten notes on stationery for all kinds of thank-you's. People appreciate it.

And remember, as my grandmother used to say, "When you make your bed, your room is 80 percent clean."

It's one major way to leave things better than you found them.

11

GROWTH

I find that the great thing in this world is not so much where we stand, as in what direction we are moving.

—-*Oliver Wendell Holmes Sr.*

B ravery and courage have become rare commodities. Young men, and older men too, seem to succumb to fear of risk. But as men, we are called to act bravely and courageously. We should use our strength to defend the weak. We should put our reputation on the line by caring for someone who needs it.

Rex Burkhead played running back for the University of Nebraska football team beginning in 2009. In 2011 he met Jack Hoffman, a seven-year-old pediatric brain cancer patient. Jack was both a Nebraska football fan and a Rex Burkhead fan. He was also was battling terminal brain cancer. Rex visited Jack in the hospital. He wrote him notes and called him by phone.

One of the football staff suggested an idea: he asked the coaches if they could let Jack run the football in the team's spring game, which was witnessed that year by more than sixty thousand spectators.

So at the right time, toward the end of the game, the offense handed the ball to Jack. With a little help from the offense, Jack ran through a hole and was encouraged by his own team and the opponents so he could continue his now-famous, sixty-nine-yard run.

Jack Hoffman made a touchdown that day. He was lifted in the air by the team while fans stood and cheered. But I don't think it would have ever happened if Rex had not stepped out with bravery and courage to plan a life-changing event for a fellow human.[7]

As a fruit of Rex and Jack's friendship, the now-famous run won an ESPY; gained Jack a visit with President Barack Obama in the White House; birthed Team Jack, which has raised millions of dollars for pediatric brain cancer; and has been viewed by more than 9 million viewers on YouTube.

Keanon Lowe, a young head football and track coach at Parkrose High School, Northeast of Portland, Oregon, faced a dire situation when he arrived at school on May 17, 2019. Lowe saw an eighteen-year-old student walk into class with a shotgun.

Almost without thinking, Lowe jumped the young man and grabbed his gun. He cleared the classroom, took the gun away, and hugged the young man until police arrived, all the while telling the young man that he cared about him, even if no one else did.

"When confronted with the test the universe presented me with, I didn't see any other choice but to act. Thank God, I passed," Lowe said. "I'm blessed to be alive and extremely happy that the students are safe. I'm not sure what's next. I haven't had the time to really think about it. But I am sure I want to be a part of the solution to school gun violence."[8]

Lowe later revealed in an interview that his quick thinking actually came from a decision from years earlier. Lowe, a receiver for the Oregon Ducks, said that his position coach asked a question of his players: If presented with an opportunity to save lives by putting your own at risk, would you do it? Lowe said the coach asked players to make the decision then because in the real emergency there would be no time for thinking. Thus, Lowe's actions.

As men, we get opportunities like this, though less dramatic, more often than we think. We're too busy to notice those in need. As Americans we are the wealthiest people on Earth. We have abundant resources that we can use to show love to our neighbors. But remember, helping others has more to do with ourselves and our growth than them.

> **Helping others has more to do with ourselves and our growth.**

Character Spurs Growth

A young Ivy League MBA graduate was interviewing with a major Wall Street firm. As the story goes, the young man had been through several rounds of interviews. He had carefully crafted a flawless resume to go alongside his impressive grade point average.

His morning interview went well, and he was feeling a bit giddy. When the interviewers broke for lunch, they went to a cafeteria. As the group went through the line, one of the execs noticed that the young man took a pat of butter and hid it under his bread plate. He snickered and said, "Nobody will miss a two-cent pat of butter."

Later in the day, after the young man had left, the group of executives gathered. They all agreed that the young man was impressive and his resume impeccable. Then the one executive recounted what he'd seen in the cafeteria line. He wondered out loud, "If the young man cannot be trusted with a two-cent pat of butter, how can we trust him with millions of dollars?"

The group declined his employment.

Does that seem trite? Should a young man who would have made millions of dollars be held in check because of a pat of butter? Of course the answer is a resounding yes.

It's been said that character is defined by what you do when no one is watching. From my time in the business world, I have found this to be true.

Most of us can be trusted when people are looking over our shoulders. But what do we do when nobody's looking? Or to put it another way, what do we do when only God is watching?

We've all seen WWJD (What Would Jesus Do?) bracelets. Some people use this question to distinguish what they believe to be good character versus bad character. I think it's more than that. If God desires that we would be motivated by his Spirit, it is impossible to use any formula to decipher when we do good and when we don't.

Character, like our bank accounts, is something that is filled up by a myriad of deposits over a lifetime. That account can be drained quickly. We've all seen the cases where, in one moment of indiscretion, a person loses his or her good reputation.

Whether we like it or not, people will make judgments on what they see, and it only takes one misstep for our lives to implode into a heap. Yet no matter how low our deposits, there is always hope. Character is something that is born out over a lifetime, not a few seconds.

In the 1970s, Chuck Colson was sent to prison. He had been one of the highest advisors to President Richard Nixon. Five men were arrested for breaking into the Democratic National Committee headquarters at the Watergate office complex.

Colson was one of seven aides to Nixon who were charged with conspiracy. After he orchestrated the Watergate cover-up, he was found out, and his life fell apart.

A political adversary, U.S. Sen. Harold Hughes (a Democrat from Iowa) contacted Colson in prison, and the two became friends. Through their conversations, Colson became a spiritual man, a man of faith. He dedicated the balance of his life to caring for prisoners and helping them in every aspect of their lives.

He founded the nonprofit Prison Fellowship through which volunteers help inmates in many ways. In the end, history judges Colson not for a series of mistakes he made while working in the White House but for his lifetime of service to prisoners and their families.

It is never too late, or too early, to start building one's character.

Be Willing to Make a Stand

As with character, a person builds his reputation brick by brick. It takes hard work. It requires standing up for "what is right" even when others won't. Each act of character ends up building a reputation. In turn, your reputation becomes a valuable asset.

Anytime an older man gives a hand up to a younger man,

A person builds his reputation brick by brick.

---

he helps. Anytime someone sticks their neck out to help someone, they place their reputation at risk. This investment, for recipients, can often make the difference between success and failure. So as we go through life, we should carefully build our reputation and invest it wisely.

Years ago, a few of our friends and I took interest in a bright young entrepreneur from Kansas State University. Toby was savvy, intelligent, and technologically gifted. He was starting a new business and needed some capital. A few of us volunteered to be on his board, and he was grateful for the help.

One of the board members, Casper, had started and sold several technology companies himself. While we all listened to Toby give his reports on a conference call, Casper alone grasped the specific market into which Toby was launching.

Things were going well for the startup. Toby and his staff had signed several significant contracts. At the next board meeting, Toby suggested that he begin hiring to anticipate the needs raised by the new contracts.

That's when Casper spoke up. "Toby, I know you have these signed contracts, but these corporations are not going to make good on the agreements. There's a storm ahead for technology companies, and these businesses will not become clients of yours."

Toby was taken aback. "But we actually have signed contracts here," Toby retorted.

The entire board, of course, sided with Casper. Much to Toby's chagrin, he heeded the warning and acquiesced, downsizing his company to prepare for the storm ahead. Sure enough things turned out exactly as Casper had predicted.

During the economic downturn, the major competitors in Toby's field closed for lack of cash flow. Months later, as the economy rebounded, Toby had fewer competitors, and his leaner company rose to the forefront.

Our friend Casper ended up being the unsung hero. He has continued his relationship with Toby, and Toby has been tremendously successful since.

Casper not only volunteered to help, but to stake his reputation on the advice he gave our young friend. To this day, Toby credits Casper for the upward trajectory of his career.

Develop Strong and Honorable Convictions

What is it about people of faith that draws us in? What about their belief in a benevolent, unseen, all-powerful force appeals to us? Paul wrote that people receive their commendation for understanding things that are not seen:

> Now faith is the assurance of things hoped for, the conviction of things not seen. For by it the people of old received their commendation. By faith we understand that the universe was created by the word of God, so that what is seen was not made out of things that are visible. (Hebrews 11:1-3)

A young man should look for people with vision in order to become a person of vision. I challenge young people to dare to believe in something, to take a stand and have strong

convictions. Be bold and courageous in the things you believe
to be true. Fail boldly.

Just after the writer of Hebrews defined faith as an assurance
of things hoped for and conviction of things not seen, he went
through and identified people of great faith: Abel, Enoch,
Noah, Abraham, Sarah, Isaac, Jacob, Joseph, Moses, and Rahab,
to name a few.

Why?

Because they chose to believe in something and to put their
life on the line for that belief.

One of my favorite stories is that of French acrobat and
tightrope walker Charles Blondin, who after stringing his wire
across the Niagara Falls asked a couple of onlookers, "Do you
believe that I can walk across on this wire and back?"

They doubted. So he took his pole for balance and walked
across the great, wide falls and back.

A crowd began to gather. Then he asked, "How many of
you believe I can walk across on my wire and back without my
balance pole?"

A few raised their hand. So he went back to the rope and
crossed the falls again, over and back.

People continued to gather, and he asked, "How many of
you believe I can push a wheelbarrow across my wire and back?"

Enthusiasm for the talented man grew stronger. About half
the crowd said they believed and cheered him on. So he walked
across with the wheelbarrow and back. By this time the crowd
was fully behind him.

"How many of you think I can do it with the wheelbarrow
and a blindfold," the man continued. The onlookers shouted
their support. And he succeeded yet again.

So he asked again, "How many of you believe that I can put a person in the wheelbarrow and walk across the tightrope and back blindfolded?" Everyone cheered and seemed to believe, until, that is, he asked for a volunteer.

This story illustrates the fickleness of humanity. It's easy for us to believe when nothing is at stake. But often what God calls us to do requires risking everything. Jesus wants us to get into His proverbial wheelbarrow.

The apostle James wrote: "But some will say, 'You have faith and I have works.' Show me your faith apart from your works, and I will show you

> **What God calls us to do requires risking everything.**

my faith by my works. You believe that God is one; you do well. Even the demons believe—and shudder! Do you want to be shown, you foolish person, that faith apart from works is useless?" (James 2:18-20).

For James, works proved the authenticity of a man's faith. Faith with no works? No way.

Let's face it, God wants us to put our skin in the game. Believing remains easy where there is no risk.

But brave and courageous faith invests all we are and all we have.

Our friend Ambassador John Richmond told us how he created a list of ten convictions that he and his wife Linda use to create their family culture. They have all thought long and hard about these topics, and I think you will enjoy them:

1. Please God.

2. Keep the ladies smiling.

3. People are always more important than stuff.

4. Speak truth and love.

5. Feelings aren't actions.

6. Know how to stop.

7. Finish the job.

8. Know your name.

9. Happen to your life.

10. Make wrong things right.

The brevity of these directions belies how profound and applicable they have been in creating the Richmond family culture. To clarify, the ladies mentioned in number two are the mother and daughter in the family, women whose respect and well being are prioritized. The imperative in number eight refers to both knowing and owning one's identity. In number nine, the family emphasizes the opposite to the familiar phrase, "Life happens".

As you can see, these general guidelines can be applied to a wide range of situations. Yet they require integrity, faith, and strong action. The Richmond kids memorized the list and refer to it day by day.

Proverbs says, "Where there is no vision, the people perish" (Pro. 29:18, KJV). In visiting other countries, I've seen this in the political leadership. Where the rulers have no faith, the people suffer.

The prophet Joel predicted that in the last days "your old men shall dream dreams, and your young men shall see visions"

(Joel 2:28). I believe God gives young men faith because they possess the chutzpah to actually carry it out.

Believe it or not, young men are uniquely qualified to see visions, to adopt grand convictions, or as Micah wrote, "to do justice, and to love kindness and to walk humbly with your God" (Micah 6:8).

When we embrace strong and just convictions, we place ourselves squarely in the sights of God. He wants us to care about justice and kindness while we walk with Him through life.

Living from the Heart

When the Lord changes people, their conversion is instantaneous. The Scriptures say that we die and are reborn into a holy image. The human heart can change in an instant, but it takes the remainder of a lifetime to get the brain to follow.

So what does it mean to be "transformed by the renewal of your mind?" (Rom. 12:2)

It means we learn to think in a new way. We take on the mind of Jesus. Although we have been changed in an instant, the transformation of the mind requires time, depth, and discipline.

What kind of discipline? It means finding and adopting truth wherever one can find it. The first and most obvious place is in the Scriptures.

We tend to forget that we have access to a printed Bible when most people in history did not. Until Johann Gutenberg invented the printing press in the early 1400s, Scripture had to be painstakingly copied by hand.

This was normally done by monks, sequestered in remote places. Millions of followers through the years have savored the

Scriptures, and children were taught to memorize large passages. They were rare treasures worth committing to memory.

Now we have a Bible in the nightstand of every hotel room. Yet we have become lazier. Memorization is difficult for us. Yet one need not memorize too many verses to understand the transformation they bring.

It is critical that young men embrace the Scriptures and develop an appetite to understand their principles. When we treasure the Scriptures in our heart, it changes us from the inside out. We remember these passages at critical times. They lead us along the way. They keep us from getting off the path, or they get us back on the path when we stray.

This is so important, that we should also seek out solid teachers of the Scriptures. I believe one of my great possessions has been the long list of teachers from whom I've been able to learn. You can find a list of them in the back of the book.

They challenged me, they taught me, they believed in me, they encouraged me. I often remember certain things that those men and women have told me, and I continue to appreciate their nuggets of wisdom, even to this day.

Wrestling with Good Questions

Ask me a good question, and I will prefer it to a thousand good answers. We think that life is about having all the right answers, especially in Western civilization. I beg to differ. A perfect answer ends a conversation. A brilliant question can carry the conversation for weeks, or months, or even years.

It's important to come up with questions for ourselves. Examples might include:

What is my purpose in life?
What makes me feel loved?
What's the main thing that's holding me back?
What are my negotiables and non-negotiables?
What breaks my heart?
Do my friends reflect who I really am?
Am I spending my money on the right things?

Limitless good questions exist, each one propelling us into a helpful conversation. I had a friend once who decided he would come up with a good question for himself each day. Every day, whenever I saw him, I couldn't wait to hear the latest. That system helped him to become curious about all kinds of things, and therefore become one of the great learners I've known.

We should ask God questions. If anything puzzles us, wouldn't it be a great knee-jerk response to ask God what His thought is? The times that I've actually done this, I find that over the next several days, I am given hint after hint as to my question. And yet with each inquiry will come another question—one that will take me deeper and draw me closer to truth.

12

WEALTH AND INVESTMENTS

The true worth of a man is to be measured by the objects he pursues.

—Marcus Aurelius

Would you like to know the quickest shortcut to success, or wealth or fame?

Work hard.

I once came up with three pieces of advice for everyone entering the workforce:

1. Do the jobs that nobody else will do. This provides job security.

2. Care for the people around you, and you will become the leader in the room.

3. Find a way to thank your boss regularly for the opportunity to have a job. This will not only improve your attitude toward your work, it will impress your superior. Gratefulness is an attractive and rare virtue.

For eighteen years, I worked as an executive in the newspaper and radio industry. Three times I was thanked for giving someone the opportunity to work for our company, which at the time employed about 130 people.

When my friend Merle heard about my formula, he insisted on a fourth part:

"Just tell them to work hard."

> **Gratefulness is an attractive and rare virtue.**

Merle had been the CEO of a Fortune 500 company, so he was no slouch on the topic. If you knew this wonderfully disciplined man, you might rightly guess that he strived hard to reach the top of his field. His advice is worth heeding.

Paul says that we should "work heartily, as for the Lord" (Col. 3:23).

So yes, we are to work hard, but we should remember that we work for an audience of One: the Almighty. This should inspire us to outwork our peers.

Please note that we are not suggesting that anyone become a workaholic. Balance is essential. But overall, when we do our work, we should do our best.

Wisdom and Money

I'll never forget explaining in great detail the highest principle of money to my six-year-old son, Dawson.

"A penny saved is a penny earned," I preached. I then explained the concept of compound interest. Any

> **A penny saved is a penny earned.**

money that we don't spend and invest remains in our possession and grows with compounding interest. Money that is spent simply disappears, and we don't see it again.

As I came to the end of my lecture, I asked him what he thought of the idea. After a pregnant pause, he looked up at me with utter certainty and announced, "Well Dad, I just think I'm a spender."

He was right. He has proven to be a spender, but after suffering a few mistakes, he's learning to manage money. I'm proud of him.

These principles of money are important:

- Never invest any money that you are not prepared to lose.
- "Never a borrower or lender be," Benjamin Franklin reminded us.
- Save money for a rainy day.

The list goes on and on.

One of my former assistants, Tara Jo, would every now and then begin a sentence by saying, "You know, my grandpa used to say . . ." Then she would utter some amazing piece of wisdom from her western Kansas Methodist heritage. Her grandfather, a banker, was clearly a monetary proverb teller.

One day I asked Tara Jo if she would collect everything she could remember her grandfather saying about money. She did so. A couple weeks later I received a four-page, single-spaced collection of her grandfather's best thoughts on money. I have attached it as Appendix A. As you can see, he clearly knew what he was talking about.

Another great source for the principles on money is the book *Money, Possessions, and Eternity* by Randy Alcorn. While I don't endorse his answers entirely, he does seem to ask all the right questions. After discussing topic after topic, Alcorn requires us to cogitate over issues we might never have considered. Every young man should read this book, not as a textbook but as a guidebook to monetary matters of life. A wise man learns the principles of money and puts them to good use.

Turn Earthly Wealth into Heavenly Gain

Anytime a person crosses the border between countries, a currency exchange is required before anything may be purchased in the destination country. So too, our currency exchanges here on Earth decide whether or not wealth awaits us in heaven.

Jesus spoke openly about those who received their reward on Earth versus those who will receive their reward in heaven. He talked about giving generously and giving in secret. Do you blab to everyone about your charitable giving?

A wealthy businessman had not only built a staggeringly successful company, he had also given generously to his community. His family name could be found on most of the giant buildings found in his city. A friend took him to lunch. During lunch, his friend posed a hypothetical situation:

"What if your chief financial officer was taking money from your company, giving it to charity, then placing his own name on the building?" he asked. The businessman's face grew red as he considered the idea that his underling would do such a thing.

Then came the stinger. His friend asked him, "So why are you using God's money to put your name on all these buildings?"

You see, it is possible to be generous and get no eternal gain. It is possible to build one's reputation on Earth by giving and profit nothing in the kingdom of God. When we give out of our abundance and we feel no sting, it benefits us little in the thereafter.

Yet Jesus gives us explicit directions about how to send our wealth forward:

Give generously.

Do it secretly.

Give in a way that hurts.

You will find an extraordinary place in eternity.

What to Manage

We talked earlier about net givers and net takers. I've found that over time net givers develop creative methods for being generous with their time, treasure, talent, friendships, energy, creativity, and reputation.

We need to be reminded that everything belongs to God. He has chosen us to be His stewards, His managers, to spread the wealth to those in need.

The art of giving is classified in the Scriptures as a spiritual gift (Rom. 12:8). That is, some people are better at it than others, but we all have room for improvement.

Giving is a spiritual gift.

As I mentioned earlier, our family's experience with trying to out give God was a flop. We couldn't give things away fast enough without them soon being replenished.

So as you consider all that you have been given, try to devise ways how you too may give to others.

In Jesus' parable of the talents (Matt. 25:13-30), the third man took the gift with which he had been entrusted and buried it in the ground. While he was given less than the others to begin with, his master later rebuked him for not using his gift.

Whether it was laziness, fear of failure, or jealousy of the size of the others' gifts that prevented him from investing his own, the man erred by wasting his potential.

The apostle Paul lists the gifts of the Spirit in 1 Corinthians 12 and 14, and in Romans 12. These are the various gifts that the Holy Spirit produces in us. You will notice that each gift is given for the betterment of others. Here is a list of the various gifts: administration, evangelism, exhortation, giving (contributing), showing mercy, prophecy, teaching, shepherding, serving, and leading.

I find it important for people to have an understanding of what their spiritual gifts are. I often ask them to look up spiritualgiftstest.com and find a questionnaire that will help them sort out what their gifts are. The questions, though a bit churchy, will actually help a person find which gifts he or she possesses. The test and scoring should take an hour, depending on your speed.

We've all witnessed the lives of people who take this idea seriously. They use their gifts, they invest them in other people, and they indeed help equip others for whatever necessity they may have.

Acquainting ourselves with our God-given gifts proves important. As we use these gifts, we prove to be like Jesus' first two examples in His famous parable of the talents. As we use these talents, they will be multiplied, and their usefulness will splash onto those around us.

13

DATING AND FAMILY

What can you do to promote world peace? Go home and love your family.

—Mother Teresa

In a phone conversation with an intern, the topic of dating arose. My young friend was interested in a girl, and she was not responding in kind. So he told her he would be available if she ever changed her mind. Little did he know that fifty other guys had said the same thing to this popular girl.

I told him he had to distinguish himself from all others. On this point, I told him he should watch the bar scene from the movie *Hitch*, when Hitch creatively introduces himself to Sarah.

He leads her in a clever conversation. Then at the precise moment she begins to gain interest, he walks away and tells her it wouldn't work. The next day he sends a courier with a package inviting her to go on a date on jet skis.

Interesting strategy, isn't it? Most guys don't realize this sort of special attention is what women want.

The interaction made me think back to an exercise we had our female interns do a few years ago. We asked them to answer four questions about dating. These were popular girls, and the answers to our questions were telling. Here are the questions and their answers:

1. Why do girls date?

    We date for a variety of reasons. We date to find what we need and what we want in a guy, to get to know someone, to have fun, to explore the possibility of a relationship, and ultimately to find a partner in life and marry.

2. How do girls want guys to ask them out on a date?

    We have all been victims of the ambiguous date request. Never attempt to ask a girl on a date by saying, "What are you doing this weekend?" Girls hate this. It is a safely played move that avoids any real risk of rejection and places the girl in an awkward position. For some guys she may be completely booked, while for another she may have all the time in the world. A girl will respect your courage in asking for something specific. If she is busy at the requested time and truly wants to go on a date, she will present alternatives. Don't be ambiguous. Take the lead, and take the risk of being rejected. Be direct, be clear, and make known what is being asked. Don't try to diminish or confuse the situation by qualifying it with "Let's hang out." Ask the girl on a date: "I'm asking you out to dinner." This makes her feel special, like you actually put thought and effort into the asking instead of making it an afterthought. Make the effort, have a plan, do it three days in advance, not the day of. Most girls enjoy the opportunity to visualize the date over a couple days and consider various options for dress. Be confident. Don't look to her for initial affirmation. Don't qualify the date or be over serious. It's just a date. It is best to ask in person, or over the phone if you don't have the chance to see her face-to-face. Anything else, such as text messaging or emailing, is a cowardly cop out. Special note: Girls in general are scared of dating and fearful of the unstated expectations. True, they are fearful of getting hurt, but even more so they are afraid of hurting someone else. Do anything you can to clarify expectations. Some of the best dates we've been on reiterated that there was no pressure. The boys were honest with their desires. They said, "I just want to get to know you."

3.   What are appropriate dating manners?
   – *Turn off the cell phone.*
   – *Pay.*
   – *Open doors.*
   – *Manners matter!*
   – *Be comfortable.*
   – *Not too much alcohol (in order to prevent the illusion of a false sense of fun).*

- *Make the date personal not prescribed. Do research but don't be overly frantic to always entertain or be flashy and impressive. Be yourself.*
- *Be a leader. End it before you want to.*
- *Walk the girl to the door.*
- *Read the situation in all contexts (what she wants, what you want, what to do, and when to end).*
- *Don't talk too much (especially excessively about yourself). Ask questions and listen to the answers. Don't just ask because you want to answer them yourself.*
- *Dress nicely. Put forth the effort.*
- *Drive safely and clean your car.*
- *Make plans. Choose a place for dinner and perhaps have several options in mind for afterward if you want her to choose.*
- *Topics to talk about: Don't get too deep and assume that you have access to personal information. Don't talk about past relationships. Not too much God talk. Have fun! Laugh! Good topics are family, friends, where you are from, and what you love.*
- *Give sincere compliments that you truly mean not just obligatory ones to fill some invisible quota.*

4. How do you decide to go on a second date? Were we impressed? Intrigued? Well taken care of? Then:
   - *Facilitate and give the girl the opportunity to respond. Allow her to say no, so she doesn't feel trapped into the following dates.*

- *Take your time; don't be overeager. Oftentimes it takes girls a while to determine how they really feel.*
- *Pursue her but don't stalk her.*
- *Be honest.*
- *Be strong enough to be rejected and know that it is hard for a girl to say no.*
- *Communication is key.*
- *Be yourself.*
- *Take it slow.*
- *Have fun!*
- *Maintain other relationships. Don't be isolating. Don't compare to other couples.*
- *Take an active interest in her friends and family.*
- *Give her freedom.*

So that's the advice that our girls gave. Because men tend to be simple, I reduced the girls' thoughts into five fundamental points:

1. Guys, **have a plan** when you call and ask girls to go out. Convey that plan to them in such a way they can answer yes or no. Include what time you will pick them up and what time you will bring them home. Give them an idea of what to wear. Use the word *date*.

2. **Call at least three days early**. Women need some time to imagine the date. They will enjoy the date much more with a little anticipation.

3. **Learn to listen.** Think up some good, engaging questions, pose them, allow the girl to answer, then follow up with related questions. As you are listening, look into her

eyes, and don't be distracted. (And for goodness sake, don't allow yourself to stare at any of her body parts.)

4. **Move the relationship along slowly**, enjoying it like a fine wine not guzzling it like a cheap beer. Remember, men are microwaves, women are Crock-Pots. Most girls will be at least two steps behind you, so be patient.

5. Most importantly, **end the date before you think you should**. You can imagine the agony of a popular girl not only having a bad date but having to endure someone who has worn out his welcome. Leave them wanting more of you, not less.

So there you have it. I'm sure others would add or subtract from my list. And I can't take credit. Our intern women educated me on this topic. Thanks especially to Amy Laughlin Williams for writing all this down.

So good luck, guys. You're entering the wild and wonderful world of man-woman relationships. Snap on your chinstrap.

Collins and Cassidy

Cassidy and Collins met in Washington, DC, during their internships there. Cassidy noticed Collins early on. Later in the year, after a deeply spiritual experience in El Salvador, Collins returned and noticed Cassidy from across the table. And although she was sick at the time, something about her made Collins say to himself, "Wow! This might really be the girl of my dreams."

They dated from a distance for a while and then broke up. The breakup was hard on them both. Cassidy described the nine-month breakup not as a desert, but as a "rich rainforest."

She waited, grew, healed, and hoped. Both she and Collins were comforted by the Scriptures:

"Unless the LORD builds the house, those who build it labor in vain. Unless the LORD watches over the city, the watchman keeps awake in vain" (Psalm 127:1).

Then came the Letter. And at the perfect time. Collins had been wondering, "Why am I not with Cassidy?" Her letter arrived in the midst of his questioning. Collins raced through the words, and at the end, he found this: "I know—and am still coming to know—a new and lasting freedom. I feel like I have nothing and everything to offer you. But if you were willing, I would give this everything I had. I'm ready to be on your team."

Wow!

A few days later and without warning, Cassidy discovered Collins once again on her doorstep, flowers in hand, arms outstretched, wanting to receive her back. A few months later, Cassidy had a ring on her finger and had moved to Columbia, South Carolina, where Collins lived and attended law school. They set a wedding date, sent out invitations, and she was choosing a gown.

Their story is one of spirit, love, patience, commitment, and integrity. I find it a good model when talking about dating and engagement.

Dare to Be a Modern-Day Gentleman

Today's men take too little time and effort to become quality gentlemen. In earlier times, a man would be given lessons on how to become one. These ideas became a cultural code of conduct.

That's not true today. If I were to quiz young men on some basic gentlemanly principles, most would fail. Many view manners as an awkward list of minor inconveniences with little purpose.

Yet the foundation of true etiquette lies with good motives. Why should we act certain ways around certain people? The code of the gentleman requires that we are motivated to treat people in such away that they feel cared for and secure.

There's a treasure chest of tips that can aid a gentleman-in-the-making. I've listed a few of the most important ones below. I think you will gain a strategic advantage if you heed them. Here are the tips:

1. Make others feel as comfortable, cared for, and secure as you are able. Perhaps the foremost example of this is where a man walks. In the days of dirty, dusty streets, the man would always walk on the street side of the woman, so as to protect her from any flying mud or elements. The exception to this rule is anytime a couple is walking into a place that is uncomfortable. Perhaps into a darkened theater. In that case, the man should lead. On other occasions, the woman should go first.

2. Always be on the alert. True gentlemen scan the horizons for opportunities to help others. Does a woman need help carrying her groceries? Does someone need to be walked out to their car? Is there ever anything that we can carry that would help out those who might most need it? This alertness is what separates the great gentleman from the good one.

3. Risk to rescue others. In any given situation, we should be alert to the safety of others, especially women and children.

4. Always let others sit down and eat before you do.

5. Dress for the authority in the room. If you research British specialists on the making of a gentleman, dress plays an enormous role. My rule is a bit simpler. I suggest that any young man should simply dress for the authority in the room. If it's a teacher wearing a collared shirt and khakis, do likewise. If you're going to church where people wear suits and ties, do likewise. If you're at the beach with your buddies, feel free to dress as they do. Otherwise, figure out who the person in charge is, and follow his or her lead.

6. Send flowers and hand-written thank-you notes often.

7. And don't forget, open and shut doors for others. You may get some pushback on this one. I do. Somehow, young women today don't see it the way we do. If someone doesn't like it, and they tell you, don't press the issue.

Do these tips feel burdensome? Sometimes. But you will gain a sense of self-confidence when you know what is expected in every situation. And, if carried out properly, you will prove to be the hero.

Prepare for Marriage and Fatherhood

Nowhere is our manhood tested so much as in marriage and fatherhood. Husbands are urged in the Scriptures to "lay

down their lives" for their wives. Try that one on for a life
goal.

I found that laying down
one's life fits into a myriad
of categories: choosing
a restaurant for dinner;
purchasing jewelry; turning

> **Nowhere is our
> manhood tested so
> much as in marriage
> and fatherhood.**

over the remote control for the TV (Yes, I realize how difficult
this is for us); discussing issues at length and with an open mind;
and giving large chunks of time, money, and energy to bless a
bride.

In fatherhood, we often find the accompanying disrespect
that comes from children. When my kids were teenagers, I took
a beating. In many cases, however, I realized later that they were
mostly right. Still, it's hard on the ego.

Through all this, we have to parent our children without
exasperating them, which means to steel our resolve and
strengthen our patience in the face of a thirteen-year-old
mouthing off. It is incredibly hard.

Usually when our group of friends has a wedding, we have
a "say-so" time with the groom the morning of the wedding.
There, we give our very best advice on marriage. The most
profound of us is my friend Grant. At each wedding, he simply
says two words: "Die early." And he doesn't mean escaping an
argument by having a heart attack. He means dying to the desire
to have your way.

As I've experimented with this, I've found that life is easier
when we learn to give in to those we love. When it comes to
conflict in the marriage, I found that one thing helps: Have a
ton of friends who will tell you when you're wrong, or right.

When the partnership with your wife turns into a one-on-one battle, it helps to have neutral third parties who know and love you both enough to speak clarity.

Oh, the pain from which my friends have delivered me!

Klaus Peter and Magda

Beth and I married in March 1984 between semesters of my graduate studies in Marburg, Germany. Like most young couples, we were frequently at odds. Being newly married we were insecure enough. Though in a new culture and language, we were on high alert.

Thankfully, we managed to make a few friends in our city, including Klaus Peter and Magda. Beth and I lived in the valley next to the Lahn River while Klaus Peter and Magda lived at the top of the hill, not too far from the town's medieval castle. Klaus Peter was older than the other friends I met, so it was natural that he acted as my marriage counselor.

So each time Beth and I fought, I would storm out the door and hike up the mountain to see Klaus Peter. He could discern when something was bothering me.

He would start by asking me how I was doing. I would respond with something nebulous like, "Well, okay." After a few probing questions, I would be dumping my truckload of feelings on him.

He patiently asked question after question to make sure I got all of my toxicity out. He listened and he listened, longer for the big problems and shorter for the lesser ones. When it was all said and done, he would turn to me and in a somewhat firm voice say, "Okay, Brad, now go buy Beth an ice cream cone and tell her you're sorry."

I've paid thousands of dollars for counseling sessions that were not nearly so helpful. And the thing was, he said the same thing every time. So each time I walked out the front door seething, I knew that in due time I would be trudging back in with an ice cream cone.

Klaus Peter has proven to be a solid friend ever since. Yet through the summer of 1984, he was an agent of reconciliation, an unlicensed therapist who prevented a marriage train wreck.

I believe we make marriage too complicated. Why do we insist on the battle when taking the humble road would be so much easier?

We know this in theory, yet we insist on stepping on the same mines over and over. Beth and I learned early on that choosing to battle over forming truces led to bitterness. We are still learning to work out our differences as quickly as possible.

Resist Pornography

I have a few short words for anyone dabbling in pornography. Stop it! Now!

If your use of pornography has become an addiction, get the help you need to rescue yourself from it. Most men operate under the illusion that what is done in private can't hurt anything. That's just not true.

Men who suffer from pornography addiction tend to also struggle with shame, insecurity, anger issues, depression, or all four. They are often not able to enjoy a healthy sex life with their wives. This addiction tends to spread to other more dangerous addictions.

For those who overcome the addiction, they find a newfound freedom, regain a zest for life, build their self-image, and enjoy a deeper intimacy in marriage.

If you have a problem with porn, you can get help from your family, your friends, a counselor, your church, or a group like Sex Addicts Anonymous. Whatever the case, get help before the addiction hijacks your life.

14

DISCIPLESHIP

When Christ calls a man, He bids him come and die. There are different kinds of dying, it is true; but the essence of discipleship is contained in these words.

—**Dietrich Bonhoeffer**

Jewish young men in Jesus' time celebrated manhood at age thirteen. At that point, the best of the best were sought out by rabbis to become their disciples. Most of us hardly realize that Jesus' disciples were a ragtag bunch. Peter, at about age eighteen, was their leader, and the others were anywhere from fourteen to sixteen years old.

Rabbis generally recruited disciples because of their aptitude. Not so with Jesus. Each disciple he picked had already been passed over by other rabbis. We know this because they had either gone into their families' business or had some other job.

So Jesus started by choosing rejects. When He approached each potential apostle, He said something to the effect of "Come, follow Me." This was the classic invitation by a rabbi to join his band of disciples. It was a great honor. Perhaps that is why the fishermen were so quick to drop their nets and follow. Did you notice nobody turned Him down?

Another distinguishing feature of the rabbi culture was the use of questions. According to the rabbis, a good question could result in any number of answers. They taught their disciples to think deeply before answering questions, and they would answer a question with a question. In math, the rabbi might ask someone, "What is two plus three?" Before the disciple answered, he would begin a logical progression: "Two plus three equals five. Eight minus three equals five. So my question in response is What is eight minus three?"

Or perhaps, a rabbi wanted to ask the disciple a particular question from the Scriptures. Remember that by this time, these Jewish youngsters had already memorized the entirety of what we refer to as the Old Testament. (Can you imagine memorizing Leviticus?) Actually, these kids had been bombarded with these writings daily for their entire existence. This is improbable for most families today.

Jesus might have asked His followers a question pertaining to a particular verse in the Psalms. The disciple would then distinguish whether he was actually talking about the verse before or the verse after what was quoted. He would go back into his backlog of verses, scan His mental database, and figure out which one applied. He would then pose a question regarding the pertinent verse that would continue the rabbi's logical progression.

Can you imagine memorizing the entire Old Testament, then being peppered with questions and required to fully comprehend what was being asked in order to answer with yet another question? Yes, it sounds confusing. (It is, and challenging.) Harvard or Yale's curriculum should be so challenging—and rewarding.

Jesus also was one of the few rabbis who had a form of "special authority." With this authority, he was allowed to look at truth from a slightly different angle. The rabbis thought of truth as solid and transparent, like a prism. When light shined on the prism, people would see the same reflection but from a different perspective. Likewise, Jesus saw the truth but from a different perspective.

So rabbis with this particular authority were allowed to pose new perspectives on the truth. When they did, they would say something like, "You have heard it said that . . . But I tell you." Sound familiar? Jesus said it.

And He lived His life as a rabbi, a teacher.

Even so, young men today have the opportunity to seek out teachers and mentors who will invest time and effort into their lives to instill truth, integrity, and spirituality into their core.

Find a Mentor and Advisor

This can be scary. How does one possibly find an able mentor and approach him about giving of his time and energy to bring a young buck along in life?

True, there are far too few men today willing to make such an investment. Yet if you seek one out and pray that the Lord will provide, I assure you, you will find the right man, or men.

As a young man, I never would have guessed that at age fifty-nine I would have a list of teachers that I'm hard-pressed to fit on one page. Collectively, each of these people has woven threads of wisdom into the tapestry that has become my life. Each person intentionally helped me grow in a significant way.

The older ones were not afraid to tell me when I was wrong. The younger ones taught me through the wealth of shared experience. Do not be intimidated if, today, your list could be tallied on one hand. That's a start.

In the meantime, read up on Jesus in Matthew, Mark, Luke, John, and Acts. You will find a wonderfully patient, kind, and wise Rabbi in Jesus of Nazareth.

While in the early stages of editing this manuscript, I sent samples around to my trusted friends and colleagues. They each came back with feedback that was both original and valuable. One friend, Bill, called his adult son after reading the section on finding a mentor.

"Nathaniel, do you have any mentors in your new photography job?" Bill asked.

"No, Dad, I don't," Nathaniel replied.

"Do you have anybody in your field who's trying to be your mentor?"

Again, his son said no.

"Well, I want you to find one. In the next month, find someone experienced in your industry with a few years under his belt. Buy him lunch. Ask him questions. See how it goes," the father encouraged.

A month later, Bill called his son to see how the mentor experiment had fared.

"Did you find a mentor?" Bill asked, ready for anything Nathaniel might report.

"Dad, I didn't just find one. I found three!" Nathaniel said.

"And how's it going so far?" his dad continued.

"Life-altering."

Not every section in the book has a test case as golden as this one. Nathaniel's experiment has caused him to grow in a new way. Key mentors and advisors tend to foster such growth.

> **Key mentors and advisors tend to foster such growth.**

A Personal Board of Directors

As Beth and I approached our forties, we were ambushed by unforeseen wealth. Beth's father had found a small fitness company in Washington State. He had gifted some stock to us, which we never thought would produce much profit. But almost overnight the value of the stock skyrocketed, and we found ourselves in a new realm, one in which we desperately needed sound counsel.

We had witnessed the benefits of money, but we had also witnessed families who were destroyed by wealth, fame, or power. The idea of having wealth for the first time frightened us. We needed help and advice, but we were not sure where to find it.

A truly original idea came to me. We had a plethora of friends who were wise and experienced in things we faced, including wealth, influence, and power. It was not difficult to pick out any number of our friends for whom we had deep respect.

We settled on appointing four "family board" members to help us through these unchartered waters. Each of the nominees accepted the job (despite receiving no pay).

Marty is a life coach who had known us for twenty-five years. Linda, the wife of a congressman, understands the political realm and is a great mother. Jerry is a successful businessman and father of six. And Bob is a close friend in our town in Nebraska.

They are people of faith, are married, have children, and are all slightly older. Because this cohort resided all over the country, we picked a hotel by a major airport for our first meeting.

We set aside two days for the exercise. I submitted our financial records to each one before the meeting. Then I wrote a detailed State of the Family address, including reports on our marriage, my job, each child, their school, our vacation plans, our plans for giving, and anything else of relevance.

What we experienced with this group was incomparable. We talked deeply about our values, convictions, beliefs, family vision, and every other important topic. We allowed ample time. We talked and thought deeply and with few distractions. Wisdom flowed from our board member friends while we scrambled to take copious notes.

Two highlights stood out that first year: One was a plan to help our children grow up understanding money and wealth while not being damaged by it. The other was an investing strategy that we desperately needed.

Through the years, these meetings became a springboard for our best decisions. Each board member has taken a deep interest in each one of our children, and we call them whenever we need advice.

Appointing a board of directors was one of the best decisions we ever made. I'm surprised that we've never heard of anyone else doing it. As you reach landmarks in your life, we highly recommend that you appoint some people to be your personal board. Take the effort seriously, and you will reap the benefits.

Read and Memorize Scripture

In 1827, Martin Luther and his closest friends, along with Philip I, Landgrave of Hesse, dedicated a theology school in Marburg, Germany. The group became distressed about the way the Church had moved. So the theology school was an attempt to train a new generation of pastors.

When I was twenty-two, I had the privilege of studying as a Fulbright student in the Philipps University Marburg school of theology. History dripped from the walls. One cannot enter the building without feeling an enormous sense of history.

Martin Luther was possessed with the idea of providing the Scriptures, accurately translated, to the common man and woman. But several barriers stood in his way, both physical and linguistic.

In 1517, as a young and inquisitive monk, Luther nailed a list of ninety-five theses, or statements, on the door of the Wittenberg Castle Church.

He had not intended to foment revolution but to realign the essence of the Church itself, and especially correct the doctrine of indulgences. (Simply put, indulgences were proxy good works borrowed from the excess of saints and sold to the masses so they could enter heaven.) The doctrine was clearly controversial.

As fate would have it, a half-century earlier, a gentleman named Johann Gutenberg invented the first movable-type printing press in about 1440 in Strasbourg, France. So for the first time, pieces of literature could be mass produced.

Yet there was another problem. Practically all the church documents were written in Latin. Even the Scriptures themselves had been translated into Latin from the original Hebrew and Greek.

Luther thought it would be a good idea to translate the Scriptures into his people's language. There was another problem. Every German village, each located a few kilometers from the next, spoke its own version of German. So the area that we now call Germany included people who spoke dozens and dozens of various local dialects.

Luther was not dissuaded. He decided literally to invent his own language. When people refer to High German today, they are actually referring to the language that Luther invented by borrowing bits and pieces of the various German dialects. He assembled the new language, translated the Scriptures from the Latin Vulgate, and took it to Mainz, Germany, to be printed on one of Gutenberg's commercial presses.

Why the long explanation?

So many of us don't realize or appreciate the incredible privilege we have to own our own Bibles. For thousands of years, the only way to experience the Scriptures was either through, (A) listening to the stories by the village sage, (B) hearing the Scriptures read from the temples or churches of their time, or (C) memorizing lengthy passages themselves.

What we have today is economical and available. Thanks to the Gideons, we can find the Bible almost everywhere, making it convenient even when we're on the road.

Perhaps you can begin to get a feel for how precious this book really is. We should treat it that way. Read the Scriptures. Enjoy the stories. Take them in. Try to relate to the crazy dysfunction of the Old Testament and be inspired by Jesus' stories and the expanding new churches in the Middle East of the first century.

The Bible is a book about love. God was kind enough to give us a manual for living that encourages us to lead fulfilling lives and prepare for the next world. Sometimes it helps to think of the Scriptures as a love letter from God because that is what they are.

These verses and passages written thousands of years before have become old friends to me. They inspire me and correct me. They teach me and take me deeper and deeper each time I read them.

So I commend them to you. Many people have shed their blood for the Bible. Esteem it. Our predecessors have worked hard to bring us the inspired texts in this form. The least we can do is pass it to the next generation.

A note to the wise: when reading the Scriptures, many a scholar gets hung up on the jots and tittles, the little minutia that can become stumbling blocks. My advice is to major

> **Read the Scriptures and major in the majors, and minor in the minors.**

in the majors, and minor in the minors. In other words do not worry so much about parts of the Bible that don't recur with consistency and hold fast to the parts that do.

Far too many people get tripped up when trying to major on the minors or minor on the majors. This is just a way of trying to make the things that the Lord deems important, important to you. Remember, He has no problem communicating.

Also, reserve judgment on the things that confuse you or cause you to doubt. In my years of reading the Scriptures, I have found that some things only become apparent after multiple readings or over time, and usually both. Or perhaps they only make sense after we have certain experiences in life.

I find that God does an amazing job in this three-dimensional, multimedia classroom that we call Earth. But above all, try to appreciate the immensity of the Scriptures, and the truth that they contain, as we allow them to impact our lives.

Learn a Trade from a Godly Person

When young men graduate from college, it usually is time to begin their career. They often come to me at these crossroads and ask how they should approach their search.

I encourage them to find a person for whom they have high respect and find a way to work for them. It does not necessarily mean it must fit within their perfect aptitudes (although that doesn't hurt). Yet what a young man will learn in this situation is how spirit, mind, and body work together to make for an effective and productive life.

In education, teachers talk about the domains of learning. The *effective* domain is leadership, learned mostly from philosophy and theology. The *psychomotor* domain involves motor learning and biomechanics. The *cognitive* domain is textbook knowledge, and the *physical* domain is all that our body requires to stay in shape and to keep coordinated.

In any given vocation, as a young man walks through life with his mentor, he can more easily pick up the aptitudes and learned behavior in all four of these domains. Perhaps it is why in the Old Testament men are taught to teach their children as they walk along the road (Deut. 11:19).

One intern of ours, Wilkes, landed a job at UPS headquarters. Another friend, an executive with the company, Keith, helped him acquire the job, then watched Wilkes as he began to grow within the UPS system.

Wilkes paid attention, cared for his coworkers, did the jobs that few others wanted to do, and remembered to thank his supervisor for the opportunity to work. Wilkes found himself promoted several times. He learned quickly, worked hard, and developed good habits.

He gained the reputation for being a wise, grateful, and helpful colleague. When Wilkes left the company to go work for his father a few years later, he brought a world of good aptitude and good attitude with him. The disciplines learned at UPS are still serving him well.

Here's some perspective on mentors. Ever wonder what it would be like to be alive at the same time as your father, your grandfather, your great-grandfather, your great-great-grandfather, your great-great-great-grandfather . . . well, you get the idea. What if you were living at the same time as all those generations?

Well, Genesis describes a time when this was true. Men lived for almost a thousand years. Imagine how many generations were living on Earth at one time! Imagine all you might learn from those who had walked the path hundreds of years before.

To consider this is to understand the power of mentoring. An older and godly mentor is uniquely equipped to teach us from his expansive database of experience.

Be a Disciple and Be Discipling

As I mentioned earlier, when my cool internship supervisor Jon challenged me to live a life of discipleship in 1981, I couldn't have imagined the richness, fulfillment, and meaning it would bring me. My world is surrounded by young men and women whom I've had the opportunity to teach and befriend.

I encourage you to invest yourself in discipling younger men. If you have not started before, start now. Start small. Perhaps with just one young man. Or even a boy. Teach them all the good things you know and encourage them to ask hard questions.

When you choose young people to teach, they need, above all, one distinguishing characteristic: they must be hungry to learn and grow. Teach them well. Fill the void. Stuff them full of rich truth. You will realize that you don't really know the material until you can teach it to someone else.

When you reach out to disciple others, you also expose yourself to all types of hurt. They will disappoint you, as Peter did Jesus. They may betray you as Judas did Jesus. They might not "get it", even as the other disciples struggled to understand. Yet even as some young men were redeemed, so will young men to whom you give yourself.

Then one day you will wake up and realize the incredible wealth that has become yours. This is not a wealth measured in dollars. It is a much finer wealth. It is the wealth of friendships.

Dawson Trotman, founder of the Navigators, made his life a life of discipleship. He encouraged others to do the same. Dawson, according to some of his friends, spoke often about how if one disciples two, and two disciple four, and four disciple eight, the entire world would be reached quickly. I heard this when I was in college. I bought in, hoping to hurry the apocalypse along.

It has been hard work, and it happened much more slowly than I thought. Indeed, my friend Doug told me once that he visited Trotman (the great mentor) when he was on his deathbed.

Doug asked Dawson, "Dawson, how many disciples have you made in your lifetime?"

Dawson took his time and thought hard.

"Two . . . no, maybe one," replied the master discipler.

Doug never forgot it. And while Dawson's estimate was probably low, one can understand what a challenge it is to teach another human well.

Yet it is a challenge worth taking.

15

PRESSING ON

If I had 300 men who feared nothing but God, hated nothing but sin, and were determined to know nothing among men but Jesus Christ and Him crucified, I would set the world on fire.

—*John Wesley*

I would like to make a few observations that can help anyone hoping to grow.

Forsake Your Comfort Zone

"You have Parkinson's disease," has reverberated in my mind since I was first diagnosed in 2013 at the Mayo Clinic in Rochester, Minnesota.

Little did I know then that this adventure would take me through a thrilling series of ups and downs that would cause me to grow as never before.

My first adventure was telling Beth, but we were both in denial.

As the next few months passed, we tried to get our brains around how this would alter our lives. My case was mild, so other people would not notice. I could still play golf, ride my bike, run, and any other number of my beloved physical activities.

Word got around. Three months after my diagnosis, I received a call out of the blue. Doug, whom I have respected for four decades, was on the line.

"Hey, Brad, I've been wondering lately if I had the gift of healing. Would you be willing to go with me to the Bethel Chapel (in Redding, California) and see if we can get you healed?"

I was flabbergasted, but how does a person turn down the unstoppable Doug? Two months later, Beth and I met Doug and his entourage at the Bethel Chapel.

For those unfamiliar with Bethel, it has become a site that specializes in miraculous healing and popular worship music. For a longtime Presbyterian, I knew I would be out of my zone.

Our hosts met with us one night and gave us a short primer on what to expect. As it turns out, there was an international conference taking place for the three days we were at Bethel. On the first day, the band played an hour of worship music. Artists painted various images on their canvases onstage. The music was upbeat, and so was the crowd. I had never seen such hand lifting before.

The leader of the worship service then came to the front and began asking people to come forward or to raise their hands if they had certain physical ailments. The people in the audience gathered around those who held up their hands, and they prayed for healing.

Then came a reporting session to detail the miracles that had taken place. Fortunately, they did not call out my ailment. Relieved, I left the building after day one.

Day two was different.

The band played the prescribed one-hour plus of worship music while the painters painted. Then when the leader came forward and began calling out ailments, he seemed to have gotten a memo from my doctor, as practically every illlness I had was listed: painful injured vertebrae in the neck, recovery from several knee surgeries, difficulty breathing, and the list went on.

The people around me somehow did not tire of my continual raised hand. They were gracious and prayed for my ailments. After a while, as I looked down the row, I saw Doug signaling me to come sit on his lap. Now I was really out of my comfort zone.

I made my way down the row and looked down at Doug's spindly, eighty-year-old legs. I thought I might break them if I dropped my two-hundred-pound body on top. Still, he insisted.

He prayed, as well as those around, that I would be healed of Parkinson's. I had a twitch that had begun in my left thumb that was a good measurement of how I was faring. After the prayer, the twitching stopped. It held still for about five minutes, then continued. That confused me. Did it just not work? Did I not have enough faith?

On day three, we were taken to the "prayer room." We were seated in chairs, as volunteers walked around the dimly lit room praying. My Presbyterian blood ran cold at this sort of display. I felt a hand on my shoulder. As I was touched, the woman began to prophesy. I don't remember all that she said, but I do remember one thing. "You will have enough time to do all the things you need to do here," she said.

Little did I know, but she had exposed my deepest fear. I had real vision for the rest of my life, and I wanted to see it through. Falling short simply did not equate.

I have carried her message with me ever since, claiming that I will have time to do the important things for which I am destined. One of those additions was becoming a grandfather to two granddaughters. I love that.

The Bethel friends told me later that I needed to believe that I was healed even though the symptoms remained. Really? I found that hard to believe.

At the end of the conference, we left wondering what had happened, if anything.

One year later, I returned to the Mayo Clinic for my annual checkup. Dr. Eric Ahlskog attended. He was one of the top Parkinson's neurologists in the country. Dr. Ahlskog took me through the regimens of testing for Parkinson's, but he did so with some extra curiosity.

Finally, after all the tests, he said, "I know a year ago we tested you and diagnosed you with Parkinson's, but now I don't see a lick of it."

"Do you have an explanation for that?" I asked with some amazement.

"No, do you?" He asked.

"I can tell you that about a year ago I went to a place called the Bethel Chapel and was prayed over. I didn't think I was healed because my symptoms still exist. What do you think about that?" I answered.

He thought for a second. "Well, I've heard of crazier things," he said.

Since that day, my relationship with Parkinson's has been more than mysterious. It doesn't seem that I'm healed, and the symptoms keep growing at a mild pace, but every time I see a neurologist he is astounded at how well I'm doing.

Thinking back on the "mystery" theme, I have to admit that I have no idea whether I was healed or not. Some doctors say so; my symptoms say otherwise. Yet I live an active and fulfilling life, as few Parkinson's patients do.

Why this story? This experience has taken me down the road of wonder. Wondering what God was doing. Wondering if He had actually done what I tried to believe He did. Wondering what the future would hold.

In the process I've learned a few things:

1. I'm grateful every morning for the parts of my body that actually work. I pray for the ones that don't.

2. I have so much to be grateful for, and I have lived a tremendous and fulfilling life.

3. My thinking has been expanded.

4. I have become more intimate with Jesus.

5. It's okay to live just one day at a time.

My latest challenge, now that I have survived the trip to Bethel and its Pentecostal ways, is that my oldest son told us that he has become a Catholic. So Beth and I have attended a number of Catholic services, surviving the discomfort but finding a love and appreciation for the people and their traditions.

Looking back, I would not want to change anything about my skirmishes with discomfort. Indeed, I am learning to embrace them.

Rest

Even God rested. After six days of creation, He took a day off. Have you ever wondered why He did that? Do you think

He was tired? Do you think He needed to recover? Or was He just lazy?

The notion that God needs rest doesn't work well in our twenty-first-century minds. We go hard, and we go long. Few things slow us down. We plow through illness, fatigue, grief. Taking time to rest could reveal our weakness, we think.

Yet God took the Sabbath day rest seriously. Perhaps that is why He modeled it for us. He knew that we, like a battery, needed time to replenish ourselves. He created sleep and rest to revive, heal, and replenish ourselves. He built it into creation, then led by example.

We need to admit that we're not good at rest, especially the idea of consistent Sabbath rest. Though it seems counterintuitive to our efficient daily production, experts tell us how vital rest is, improving our ability to learn, recover, and remember. We need to find a way to incorporate rest into our otherwise chaotic existence.

Play

We need play. It is therapeutic for our bodies. It sharpens many of our hand-eye skills; it builds unity with others (or disunity, depending on the opponent), deepening bonds between us and our friends or family, or even our foes. If you haven't found ways to enjoy play, begin carving out time now. It doesn't get easier. Establish play in your routine early because there will be no room for it later.

Exercise

Studies continue to prove that exercise serves as the proverbial fountain of youth. Few things prolong our mental and physical fitness more than regular exercise. You should seek a health regimen that incorporates a healthy diet and exercise.

There exists no shortage of information on the above subjects. These are things that have been written about exhaustively. There are vegetarian diets, vegan diets, paleo diets, and keto diets, to name a few. There are extreme exercise routines, low-impact routines, water exercises, indoor exercises—just about everything for everyone. We should all find something that works for us and do it. It helps if you do it with a friend. Not only will you be more regular about it, but you will also enjoy the camaraderie. Find some principles that you believe in, and that you can incorporate into your routine.

Balance comes from within. If you are centered internally, you will gain a noticeable advantage in life.

In Closing

If you rushed through this material, you should feel as if you were attempting to sip from a fire hydrant. I realize that skipping over these topics so quickly keeps you in the shallow end, but this is a collection of wisdom that we hope will provide inspiration throughout your lifetime.

We hope it is something you will come back to again and again and read one section at a time, ruminating on topics that inspired you. These are topics that you will slowly process and absorb throughout your life. You will understand them on a deeper level as you grow in knowledge and wisdom.

I hope you enjoyed these bits of wisdom. Truly, I sometimes wish I could go back and try life again, with these things in mind. It is my hope and desire that they inspire you the way they have me.

I pray that we all will finish this race well.

APPENDIX A

TARA JO'S GRANDPA ON FINANCES
February and March 2005, right after Grandpa died

TOPIC	SCRIPTURE
Own the cattle	Ps. 50:10-12
Tithing	1 Cor. 13:3, 2 Cor. 9:7, Acts 20:35, Pro. 3:9
Sparrow	Ps. 84:3
Render to Caesar	1 Cor. 4:2, Luke 16:1-2
Debt	Rom. 13:8, 1 Cor. 7:23, Pro. 22:7
True riches	Luke 16:11
Two masters	Matt. 6:24
Contentment	Phil. 4:11-12
Ownership	1 Chron. 29:11-12, Ps. 24:1
Supplier	Phil. 4:19, Matt. 6:33, 1 Kings 17:4-6

TOPIC	SCRIPTURE
Talents	Matt. 25:14-30
Treasure	Matt. 6:21
Widow's mites	Mark 12:41-44
Prodigal son	Luke 15:11-32
A test	1 Cor. 3:12-14, 1 Tim. 5:8
Work ethic	Col. 3:23-24, Exod. 20:9, 2 Thess. 3:10-12
Responsibilities	Eph. 6:5-9, Col. 3:23
Investing	Gen. 41:34-36
Gambling	Pro. 28:20
Rich young ruler	Luke 18:18-23

- Money is about attitude—or a good reflection of it.
- Hold money loosely, because it isn't yours anyway. But care for it like it is. It's the Lord's.
- Make more than you spend. Don't spend what you don't have.
- Tithe at least 10 percent. It is the most fun part of a budget.
- Save 10 percent of paycheck.

- For a couple, try and live off of one paycheck. It might not happen but try to keep it close.
- Don't borrow except for an appreciating asset like a house. I shouldn't have borrowed for my pickup.
- Pre-planned expenses: Be patient, wait. You'll appreciate it more. Sleep on it at least one night.
- Risk (especially at a young age), but risk wisely. Risk on your retirement and on money you don't really need.
- Keep good credit. Don't pay your bills late.
- Inheritance is a gift not a right. Call it a "gift" or "blessing." I feel like Grandpa had no strings attached to my gift. It was to bless me, for he saw he didn't need it at that stage in his life, and he "d--n sure" didn't want the government to get his hard-earned money or the portion that he felt wasn't theirs. He not only gave to his children, but to the grandchildren, because I believe he saw that his children had enough for themselves. He gave each grandchild $5,000 at 8th grade graduation to help us start saving for college! That was important to him, since he had no education.
- Giving toward building God's kingdom: Where is the Lord directing you to give? Where is he already working? Don't give just because they are your friends or it is a good organization. You need conviction.
- Appear as if you have less than you do. Make it my conscious effort.
- Don't say, "I can't afford ____" or "I'm broke." The latter is a state that will change, and the former is a consequence of your choices and not really true.

- Budget: Make it for yourself not someone else. Be accountable to it. Write down every penny spent for at least a month and periodically after that to see how you might be wasting your money, or to find out what you are really buying. Consider the envelope system, where you place the necessary cash for each weekly line item in a designated envelop. When the cash is gone, you're done, unless you "borrow" from another fund.
- Saving is a choice.
- Name brand or off-brand, both could be good or you might prefer to spend a little more for the name brand.
- Dad said to me, "I trust your mother," when we spoke of the family finances. He is clueless about them, and both parents are okay with it. Mom knows she has to be responsible back to Dad, so she can't squander everything.
- Grandpa and Mom don't seem to live in fear of money or the responsibilities that come with it. Grandma and I tend to, hence we hold on too much.
- Money doesn't define character.
- Theory: Everyone has a vice he or she spends money on i.e. travel, boots, hats, coats, cars, etc. Keep it under control.
- Be above reproach and ethical even if it is ten cents. You're better off cheating yourself than someone else.
- It's best if Mom can stay home with the kids. You might not have the newest car or best vacation, but no one will regret the time spent together.

- Don't buy a new car—it depreciates so rapidly.
- Homemade and home cooked is better tasting and cheaper. It makes a restaurant more special.
- Spend on relationships: trips together and connecting with friends.
- Have a few friends or family know your finances, your philosophy, dreams, situations, and vices. They make good advisors.
- You can't take it with you, so bless others.
- Money can be divisive if either party lets it.
- Don't throw your net worth around by the way you dress or what you drive.
- Money is talked about maybe less than sex.
- An able body shouldn't be lazy.
- Take pleasure in working.
- The fun is in earning money.
- Whether you have money or don't have money, you still have to deal with it.
- Don't fear money or the lack of it. The Lord is in control.
- Be the one who buys every once in a while, even if the other party can afford it.
- Don't clutter your life with things.
- Money isn't the answer, only a means.
- Buy things at the church bazaar to help the church not because you need the item.
- The shoeshine stand is not an uppity thing but an honest way for a person to make money. Do them a favor and get your shoes shined.
- Tip at least the norm. If the service is really good, tip more.

- Reconcile your statements.
- Gambling: Definitely don't risk more than you can afford to lose.
- You are worth the $1,200 dress, but you might be eating peanut butter and jelly for a while.
- A debit card is good reality plastic.
- Have a credit card with a low limit, and only one. Have someone ask you how you are doing with it. Most importantly, pay it off at the end of each billing cycle.
- Have three to six months of expenses saved.
- Care for widows and orphans and not just with money.
- Care for your family. The Lord made the family unit.
- Don't be pushed into buying something you don't want or need.
- Shop around.
- Wait for the sale.
- Use rebates and discounts.
- Think before loaning money to friends or family.
- Give a little, take a little. It all comes out in the wash. Don't be such a penny pincher that you can't drop a few dollars now and then without someone owing you.
- It's cheaper to eat at home plus saves on gas.
- Pay an extra mortgage payment a year.
- Be a month ahead on bills or your pay cycle.
- Save for known expenses like Christmas gifts or car insurance.

- It's okay to pay for some things, such as an automatic car wash, house cleaning, or oil change.
- Put money into a Roth IRA.
- Make your first check after payday be for tithe.
- Tithe off your gross income.
- Don't give expecting God to bless you back financially. Give out of pure motives.
- You appreciate things more if you have to pay for them, like college.
- Start understanding the basics of finances like taxes, checkbook, saving, and tithing while in high school.
- Make family more important than money.
- Dad comments how he has never lost a harvest because he rested on Sunday. Observe the Sabbath. The physical and mental respite will do you good.
- Success in life: Have no regrets in regards to money. Your focus should be on bringing people closer to the Lord and loving them well.
- Money comes, it goes, and it comes again. (If you are working, that is.)
- Don't save only to "live" in the future. You need to enjoy yourself now too.

APPENDIX B

MY HALL OF FAME

"A teacher affects eternity; he can never tell where his influence stops."

—**Henry Adams**

"Leadership is not about titles, positions or flowcharts. It is about one life influencing another."

—**John C. Maxwell**

I t humbles me when I think of all the people the Lord sent who have influenced me for good. The following people (1) had a major influence on me, (2) were intentional about it, (3) were older, mostly, (4) had authority over me in some way, and (5) were not afraid to tell me when I was wrong.

Joel Anderson
Mike Antonio
Gene Armstrong,
   uncle
Bess Armstrong,
   aunt
Bill Barrett
Pepper Bullock
Rick Carus
David Coe
Doug Coe
Jan Coe
Jon Coe
Tim Coe
Jack Campbell
Dixie Cavner
Marty Colladay
Chuck Colson
Brad Colerick
Jim Dawson
Bob Dudley
Les Duly
Grant Ellis
Robert Fitzgerald
Nels Foerde
Sam Fuenning
Lilian Fuenning
John Gelvin
Al Gillet
Doris Gillet
Gerard Helminiak
Shelly Helminiak

Don Jelinek
Jan Jonker
Jerry Jonker
Steve Jurgens
Richard Halverson
Sam Hines
Jim Hiskey
Lorraine Hiskey
Stan Holmes
Jerry Huse
Herb Jost
Jerry Klingman
Robert Knoll
Jim Lightbody
Carol Madison
George Madison
Robert Manley
Dave Connell
Robert Milligan
Cynthia Milligan
Paul Nauman
John Nicholson
Bill Nottage-Tacey
Gary Oliver
Beth Olsen, wife
Chuck Olsen, dad
Joyce Olsen, mom
Mel Olsen,
   grandfather
Sarah Maren Olsen,
   grandmother
George Pasek

Stan Parker
Lyston Peebles
David Peter
Georg Pflueger
Klaus Peter Radtke
Magda Radtke
Emil Reutzel
Lee Rooker
Lou Schwartz
Liz Schwartz
Marty Sherman
Anne Sherman
Irene Skeen,
   grandmother
Ralph Skeen,
   grandfather
Barbara Skinner
Tom Skinner
Jim Slattery
Linda Slattery
Parker Smith
John Staggers
Clarke Stevens
Vern Steiner
Bob Wade
Becky Wagner
Ken Wagner
Gene Walter
Dave Weaver
Roland Werner
Elke Werner

INDEX

D

E

F

G

H

I

J

L

M

ENDNOTES

1   Alice G. Walton, "New Studies Show Just How Bad Social Media Is for Mental Health," Forbes, November 16, 2018, https://www.forbes.com/sites/alicegwalton/2018/11/16/new-research-shows-just-how-bad-social-media-can-be-for-mental-health/#36a2b9e07af4.

2   William Barclay, *The New Daily Study Bible, The Gospel of Matthew, Vol. II,* "God's Standard of Judgment" (Louisville: Westminster John Knox Press, 1975), 381.

3   Sandra Bullock as Leigh Anne Tuohy in *The Blind Side,* directed by John Lee Hancock, produced by Broderick Johnson and Andrew Kosove, released November 20, 2009.

4   Oswald Chambers, *My Utmost for His Highest,* rev. ed. (New York: Dodd, Mead, & Co, 1963. First published in Oxford in 1927), December 7 reading.

5   Greg Spencer, "Real Presence and the Image Consciousness Fairy," *Boundless,* a Focus on the Family community, September 27, 2007, https://www.boundless.org/adulthood/real-presence-and-the-image-consciousness-fairy/.

6   Lorie Johnson, "The Deadly Consequences of Unforgiveness," CBN News, June 22, 2015, https://www1.cbn.com/cbnnews/healthscience/2015/june/the-deadly-consequences-of-unforgiveness.

7   "7-year-old Jack Hoffman scores a 69-yard touchdown," *Washington Post,* September 24, 2019, https://www.washingtonpost.com/video/sports/7-year-old-jack-hoffman-scores-a-69-yard-touchdown/2019/09/24/bdbd8fc4-89e4-4bb3-b046-0671367748c6_video.html.

8   Amir Vera, "Former college football standout reportedly tackles gunman at Oregon high school," CNN, May 20, 2019, https://www.cnn.com/2019/05/17/us/former-oregon-football-player-tackles-gunman/index.html.

CPSIA information can be obtained
at www.ICGtesting.com
Printed in the USA
JSHW020410260220
4446JS00001B/1